A Comparative Guide
To Classification Schemes
For Local Government
Documents Collections

A Comparative Guide
To Classification Schemes
For Local Government
Documents Collections

Russell
Castonguay

Greenwood Press
Westport, Connecticut • London, England

Library of Congress Cataloging in Publication Data

Castonguay, Russell.
  A comparative guide to classification schemes for
local government documents collections.

  Bibliography: p.
  Includes index.
  1. Classification—Books—Government publications.
I. Title.
Z697.G7C37   1984   025.4'602517'34   83-26594
ISBN 0-313-24208-9 (lib. bdg.)

Z
697
G7
C37
1984

Library of Congress Catalog Card Number: 83-26594
ISBN: 0-313-24208-9

First published in 1984

Greenwood Press
A division of Congressional Information Service, Inc.
88 Post Road West
Westport, Connecticut 06881

Printed in the United States of America

10 9 8 7 6 5 4 3 2 1

Contents

Illustrations

Preface

Evaluative research may often be a valuable tool for professionals, since it offers side-by-side comparisons of competing systems of operation. Comparative evaluation contributes to the selection processes used in making decisions and sometimes points the way toward a new and better system. With these ideas in mind, the pages that follow provide a general, comparative discussion of local government information, local government documents classification schemes, and document indexing methods. While the nature of the discussion principally relates these topics to local documents collections in public libraries, other types, such as university libraries, are also included. Indeed, so much of the discussion is directed toward the nature of the individual collections, without prejudice toward any one type of library, that readers should have no difficulty in relating the material to their own situation.

In Chapter II of this book, a number of published classification schemes for the organization of local government documents are evaluated. The purpose of the evaluations is to point out the major principles of organization in each scheme, the scheme's objectives, its special features, and any perceived problems, all with an eye toward using such schemes to organize a collection of local government documents.

Although the classification schemes to be considered will be the central foci of the book, those sections are preceded by a discussion of elements commonly associated with the maintenance of local government documents collections, all of which are of some consideration in the process of selecting a classification scheme for their arrangement.

The evaluations of individual classification schemes, which comprise the major portion of the book, are an attempt to gather in one place, descriptions and comment pertaining to a number of arrangements for the organization of local government documents. This is a neglected area in the local government documents literature. It is hoped that this compilation will be of benefit to those libraries, librarians, and information specialists who want an understanding of alternate ways of organizing their local government publications, and thereby will have served as a complement to the existing literature.

The inclusion of the seventeen schemes reviewed in the book was based on the availability of information in published form about each classification, as well as the ability of each to be used in a practical setting.

In instances where the classification scheme in question had not been described by any officially designated name, the textual references have employed familiar names of the author's own choosing. Thus, the classification developed at the University of Texas at El Paso Library becomes the UTEP Classification, a convenience factor that the author hopes offends no one.

Throughout the text, in order to avoid repetitive terminology, the terms local government documents, local documents, and municipal documents have been used interchangeably, as they often are in academic literature. The term municipal documents might suggest a somewhat narrow focus to some readers, particularly in localities where county government and regional organizations play important parts in local affairs. Generally, the widest scope of publications falling within the boundaries of local government documentation can safely be said to include documents produced by governments and organizations below the state or provincial levels. Individual communities might have a narrower view, depending on circumstances.

It came to light during preparation of the book that the Frances Loeb Library at Harvard University's Graduate School of Design had abandoned their in-house subject classification in favor of the Library of Congress Classification. This was also true of the Bureau of the Census Library. The benefits that accrue from using the Library of Congress Classification are numerous, particularly for large libraries. The move away from these in-house classifications by larger libraries does not mean, however, that the schemes they have left behind are of no value to the library that has to provide original cataloging and classification for a moderate-sized collection of local government documents. It is entirely possible that the use of microcomputers in many small libraries could reverse the trend toward using Library of Congress Classification for small special collections. If libraries use their computers to organize small collections, then in-house classification schemes might multiply. The CODOC System, which is computer coded, appears to be dormant in terms of growth at the moment. It will be interesting to note whether or not the spread of computers into small libraries has any effect on the growth of the CODOC System, vis-à-vis the Library of Congress Classification.

Following the discussion of the classification schemes, the book presents a case for enhanced retrieval of the information contained in local documents. A suggestion is offered for content indexing of documents, using either manual or automated indexing techniques.

Finally, an extensive, annotated bibliography has been compiled to help the reader locate additional scources of information. The bibliography has been supplemented with a subject index to assist the reader's pursuit of more information, as many books and articles cover more than one related topic.

A Comparative Guide
To Classification Schemes
For Local Government
Documents Collections

1

Local Government Documentation

Within the past six years, a number of papers have been published on the subject of local government documentation. Originating far afield, such reports as those issued by the British Library's Research and Development Department, the Danish government's Ministry of the Interior, and the Illinois Regional Library Council are among the bellwethers signaling a growing interest in local government documents.[1] This interest is shared by the governmental agencies that issue the documents, as well as by the people and institutions whose activities are affected in one way or another by their issuance. The reports and papers examining the condition of local government information frequently mention the public library as playing a role in either the provision, collection, or dissemination of such information.

The suggestions for public library involvement do not imply that public libraries have ignored information on the local government level. Indeed, many libraries have not. The Illinois Local Documents Project, which was overseen by the Illinois Regional Library Council, found that twenty out of eighty-three libraries surveyed in the six-county Chicago metropolitan area maintained archival collections of local government documents dating to 1920.[2] This is a good indication that some substantial collections exist. What the reports are proposing, however, is that all public libraries should be aware of the growth in local government publication, as well as the increasing interest in such documentation. The latter is an outgrowth of an increasing information consciousness within societies, particularly at the local level.

Lesley Grayson, Research Officer at Polytechnic of North London, has written of the increased output of local government information, which has come about in part by an increased demand among governments and constituents, as well as by the implementation by municipal governments of new management techniques, such as the corporate approach to problem resolution, and cooperative planning. In a related trend, Heywood T. Sanders, of the International City Management Association, has offered evidence that city governments in the United States have become more businesslike because of a trend toward the adoption of more council-manager governmental structures, particularly in the Western states.[3]

Of information consciousness and changing government attitudes, Grayson has cited as one cause the additional data now required of local governments by central governments. Grayson has given as other causes the increasing numbers and severity of urban problems, the need for more information about constituents, and the move away from purely physical approaches and toward corporate solutions to planning problems. Corporate problem resolution not only requires manipulation of data in a different way, but has a greater likelihood of resulting in some form of published document.[4]

The information needs of local government are further complicated because local documentation is an area of publication with a tradition of limited bibliographic control, irregular publication, small press runs, random acquisition practices, poor publicity, uneven reference service, and nonstandard archival retention. When the local public library becomes involved in this unsophisticated communication network, it often finds no guidelines or service models to examine as frames of reference when establishing its own role in the local government information network. There is a possibility that in larger cities, the Municipal Reference Library, if there is one, may serve as a model, as well as helping the public library to define its role in the provision of local government information.

DEFINITIONS

One excellent result of the Illinois Local Documents Project was the creation of a handbook for organizing a local government documents collection.[5] Included in the handbook were definitions of local documents, local records, and local history materials. The definition of local government documents was as follows:

Local documents are those materials issued by local governmental agencies and their subunits, including municipalities, counties, townships, villages, special districts, school boards, park districts, and the like. Typical types of local documents include municipal codes, building codes, zoning ordinances, annual reports of agencies, financial reports, minutes and proceedings of boards and committees, reports of committees and commissions, and any similar materials produced by governmental units.[6]

This definition compared favorably with the definition used by the Greenwood Press *Index to Current Urban Documents* program, as described by Michael Shannon, Librarian at Herbert Lehman College Library, City University of New York. The definition also is compatible with a list of the most important documents commonly produced by a typical Canadian municipal corporation, as described by F. Brent Scollie of the National Library of Canada's Subject Analysis Division. All three definitions differ somewhat in terminology and inclusiveness, but essentially describe those publications produced by the city or town corporation, its laws, departmental and agency reports, and the publications of special bodies, the latter sometimes including nongovernmental agencies.[7]

Nakata's definitions in the Illinois Local Documents Project's handbook are best for their differentiation between local documents, local records, and local history materials. The handbook also suggests with specificity, those local documents which might constitute a core collection.

ACQUISITION

Acquisition of local government documents has long been difficult, principally because of the manner in which these documents are published, announced, and distributed. Often the only evidence of a specific document's existence is reference to it by local authorities or mention in the local press. This is particularly true if it involves a document prepared for internal use within one agency or department. Therefore, it is imperative for local document collection purposes, that the librarian responsible for acquisitions have good knowledge of the structure and internal operations of the local government in his or her own locale. This knowledge is the librarian's first step in bibliographic control and is made necessary by insufficient bibliographic coverage of publications at the local level. Familiarity with the operations of local government helps the librarian to know which governmental agencies are likely to have specific types of information on file, identifying which agencies generate publications, and assists in the classification of the documents if the documents are classed by issuing agency or by agency function. A majority of the published documents classification schemes group all documents by the archival principle of provenance, which is an arrangement by the name of the agency or department that issues the publication.

Knowledge of the local government's structure, while identifying areas of document collection, still does not make acquisition easy. Even in cities with municipal reference libraries, such as New York, acquisition is far from comprehensive. A state audit found that the New York City Municipal Reference Library obtained only 60 percent of known city documents.[8] Other factors affecting acquisition have been described by William C. Robinson, a member of the Graduate School of Library and Information Science faculty, University of Tennessee at Knoxville. The results of Robinson's survey of public and academic libraries in Tennessee found that acquisition was difficult because of (a) the lack of information about available publications, (b) copies of documents being out of print or difficult to obtain from the issuing agency, (c) a lack of effective records management programs, (d) irregular publication schedules, and (e)

informal methods of publication, such as photocopying.[9] Robinson found
that cost is another significant factor in any library's decision to collect
local documents.[10]

Some librarians who have been involved in the often difficult acquisition
process have offered some advice on easing the procedure. Richard Moore,
Library Director at Southern Oregon State College, has suggested ways in
which the public library may approach its local government documents
acquisition problem in addition to discussing the impact of Public Law 93-
502, the Freedom of Information Act, which provides opportunities for ex-
change of information between federal and local governments prior to project funding.[11] Moore suggests the librarian in charge of collecting the
documents establish a good rapport with public agencies and explain that
the provision of the documents will assist the library in its dissemination of
information to the public. Other means of acquiring documents involve
contacting newly elected municipal officials and explaining local documents
library reference service, watching newspapers for announcements of
reports, and persuading city and town agencies to announce in the local
newspaper that documents are available at the public library.[12] Other
commonly used techniques often mentioned in journals and books are
getting on the mailing lists of local offices and agencies and visiting local
city or town offices periodically to talk with local officers. Even if the local
officials are unavailable, secretaries are often excellent sources of information about operations. Establishing a permanent mailbox for the library
in various city agencies to collect unpublished interoffice memoranda and
ephemera is also highly recommended. The library might also want to
consider providing a current awareness Selective Dissemination of Information service to local officials in return for their cooperation in sending
copies of documents to the library. The Subject Index to the Annotated List
of Sources Consulted of this book contains citations to articles that discuss
Selective Dissemination of Information services for local government
officers.

Starting a local documents checklist also is an excellent beginning
toward better bibliographic control. The Los Angeles Municipal Reference
Library, for example, has compiled a checklist of city publications issued on
a regular basis and uses it for acquisition purposes.

A library might also consider becoming a depository for local
government documents. Having official depository status sometimes makes
it easier to acquire documents from city agencies. Depository status may be
voluntary, based on an oral agreement, or legislated. Legislated status is
usually the preferred form, as it gives the library a legal leg on which to
stand when going after the documents. As the City-County Library of
Sacramento, California, found, a depository ordinance eliminates the
whimsical nature associated with voluntary and oral deposit agreements
with elected officials, particularly when those officials are subject to a

change of heart.[13] The Sacramento City-County Library, which is a designated depository, receives two copies of each publication issued by city and county agencies.[14]

For those libraries interested in pursuing depository status, the Government Documents Association of New Jersey reports that the American Library Association's Government Documents Round Table Work Group on Model Legislation " . . . has been collecting local ordinances establishing depositories for county and municipal publications."[15] Two dozen ordinances had been collected as of the date of the published announcement, which also reported that statewide legislation existed in California, Nevada, and Texas.[16] The degree to which the statewide legislation varies is in need of explanation. For example, California Government Code, sec. 12226, *allows* cities or counties to send to the state archives copies of or original items having historic interest or value. Consent must be given by the Secretary of State before the transfer can be made. In contrast, Nevada Revised Statutes, secs. 378.150-378.200, created a State Publications Distribution Center within the Nevada State Library. Paragraph 3 of Sec. 378.180 *requires* all city, county, and regional agencies to deposit one copy of each of its publications with the State Publications Distribution Center. Section 378.190 allows any library in the state to be designated a depository. The Nevada legislation could easily serve as a model for other states wishing to tighten bibliographic control of local documents, as well as improving access.

Some pros and cons of depository legislation have been examined by Michael Shannon:

It has been undoubtedly true that there remains no way to enforce compliance by city departments with such ordinances, for in most instances the legislation has been loosely written, chiefly conveying an unenforceable intent. . . .

Yet even though deposit legislation remains generally weak such ordinances are highly recommended, for they are helpful in focusing attention on single, designated collections, and they provide libraries with some kind of a "handle" with which they may demand copies of documents from city fathers. . . . existing law has its own aura, with which the officials may be awed, thereby turning over to the library one of those hard-to-find copies of a city study.[17]

Shannon also mentioned that Terry Weech conducted a survey of local documents in Iowa's academic and public libraries in 1979. Only nine of the responding libraries were depositories.[18] Deborah Babel made a nationwide survey of fifteen public libraries and fourteen university libraries in 1976, as part of her master's paper in library science at the University of North Carolina, Chapel Hill. Babel found six public libraries reported having depository status, four of those six being partial depositories. Four other public libraries were either unofficial depositories or attempting to gain formal status. Only one university library reported having depository status for local publications.[19] Even though Babel's sample was very small and yielded a below-average rate of response, her methodology was sound, thereby presenting the possibility that there exists a higher percentage of local depositories than Weech's survey might indicate. This area is one of the many affecting local documents that needs further statistical inquiry.

However rapidly or slowly libraries are moving toward depository status to ease the acquisition of local government documents, it is curious to note that in 1933, Rebecca B. Rankin, addressing the American Library Association's Committee on Public Documents, recommended that city officials deposit copies of their publications with both the local public library and the Library of Congress, as a means of improved bibliographic control.[20]

BIBLIOGRAPHIC CONTROL

Bibliographical control of local government documents can be summed up very briefly in two short sentences: historically, it has been poor; it is improving slowly.

The haphazard bibliographic control of local documents principally has been caused by at least two factors: limited interest in them, and differing opinions over which agency should collect and organize them. The growth in interest of local documents, because of increased federal and local government interaction, already has been described. Other factors contributing to this increasing tide of public interest are: growth in urban studies at the academic level, particularly since the 1960s; increased use of quantitative methodology in the public and academic sectors; such laws as the Freedom of Information Act, supporting the public's right of access to government information; and the idea that effective government depends upon the ready availability of information, this latter development signaling a shift in government's thinking of information as unessential matter to be distributed to the public as freebies. Additionally, various local pressure groups have extracted information from local government, and organizations like the International Conference of Mayors Association have urged city halls to make local information available.

Bibliographic control, however, has not kept pace with interest. One major stumbling block has been whether organized bibliographic control should be centralized or decentralized. As an issue, bibliographic control knows no national boundaries. The same question of centralized versus decentralized bibliographic control has been raised in Canada and the United Kingdom, as well as in the United States. *Canadiana*, the national bibliography of Canada, the *British National Bibliography*, and the *National Union Catalog*, as centralized bibliographic sources, all have relatively poor coverage of local documents. In Canada, it has been recommended that the National Library of Canada (NLC) should increase the coverage of local documents in *Canadiana*. Cynthia Durance, Director of the Cataloguing Branch of the NLC, has reported the recommendation of the Canadian Task Group on Cataloguing Standards that the NLC should study the feasibility of adding to the national data base, the local and provincial document records processed by nonconventional systems, such as CODOC.[21] CODOC is a computer data base of local and provincial government documents, maintained in a format compatible, upon modification, with the Library of Congress's MARC format. CODOC, which began as an in-house documents-processing system at the University of Guelph, is discussed in more detail later in this book. By including information from CODOC's records, and from the records of other nonconventional documents listings, the NLC would create a national local documents data base. The bibliographic records from this proposed data base would be made available in machine-readable form, and indexes to the records would be issued in print or microform.[22] Durance, however, did not state explicitly whether the proposed national data base for local documents would be incorporated into *Canadiana*. The implication, however, was that there would not be an integration of records, as the two data bases would not be compatible.

In Canada's case, if such a national bibliography of local government documents comes to pass, it will have done so because of cooperative efforts by CODOC and others at the regional and local levels to gather the information. Of course, the leadership and resources available from a central bibliographic entity, namely the National Library of Canada, cannot be overlooked.

In the United States, it is hard to say exactly how, or if, orchestrated bibliographic control of local documents will come into being. There are, however, some trends afoot which seem to be pointing the way.

Bibliographic control of local government documents in the United States appears to be going in two directions. The first of these appears to be regional control. States with state libraries actively interested in collecting these documents will begin serving as one source of regional control. The State Publications Distribution Center at the Nevada State Library, mentioned earlier, is one example. Regional computer networks offer another arena where bibliographic control may come into being for those libraries that have computer access and that choose to place their holdings into the data base. For example, Yuri Nakata, who headed the Illinois Local Documents Project, reported that the Chicago Transit Authority was beginning to enter its documents into the Online Computer Library Center (OCLC) data base.[23]

Regional documents libraries, or networks of libraries to collect local documents, were suggested in 1933 by Rebecca Rankin to the American Library Association's Committee on Public Documents, as mentioned earlier. Throughout the years, that suggestion has been echoed by other writers in the field, such as Hollingsworth, Fry, and Shannon.[24] Shannon has said that centralized checklists:

can avoid the repetitive duplication of effort and inconsistencies in processing by many libraries in a decentralized approach. An examination of existing checklists produced by a variety of smaller libraries will frequently show lack of comprehensiveness, weak depository arrangements, confusion over main entries, duplication of resources and underutilization of research.[25]

Regional checklists, presumably, would incorporate the attributes that Shannon has connected with a centralized bibliographic effort. Regional attempts at bibliographic control certainly could be a step on the way to centralized records at the national level.

In spite of the arguments for regional checklists, the second direction in which bibliographic control of local government documents seems to be moving is toward a national checklist, namely, the formerly mentioned *Index to Current Urban Documents*, which is published by Greenwood Press. The index lists the publications from municipalities of just about any size, although most of the communities that are covered by the program have populations in excess of 100,000. Paper copies of documents submitted by municipalities, usually through their local public library systems, are reproduced in microfiche by Greenwood Press. Cities and towns that submit their documents receive a microfiche copy in return, along with the original document. Duplicate microfiche are available for sale to users of the index.

Mary Kalb, editor of *Index to Current Urban Documents*, has worked to resolve some of the common complaints about the index, such as poor choices of subject headings and insufficient cross-references. In 1975, beginning with volume four of the *Index*, a new subject headings list, specifically designed for the program, was implemented. It was published as *Urban Affairs Subject Headings*. A revised and expanded edition was published in 1983 as *Contemporary Subject headings for Urban Affairs*. In the subject headings list "see also" references were used primarily between terms that were separated alphabetically, since the vocabulary was designed to bring related aspects of a subject together in an alphabetical fashion. Use of *Urban Affairs Subject Headings* allows more entries under subject, rather than by type of document, correcting another common complaint.[26]

Index to Current Urban Documents functions largely through participation by local public and academic libraries, which serve as collection points for the documents of counties, regions, cities, and towns. As such, *Index to Current Urban Documents* serves as a national centralized alternative to regional data networks for those libraries and institutions having either no access to automated systems or no regional bibliographic center. Therefore, while the group of libraries involved in regional bibliographic control of documents does overlap with the group participating in the national checklist, the two groups are not necessarily identical.

In 1973 Peter Hernon, a faculty member at Simmons College Graduate School of Library and Information Science, wrote of spotty coverage of the documents from cities participating in *Index to Current Urban Documents.*[27] Improved coverage of participating cities will come about when steps are taken at the local level to tighten bibliographic control, such as the designation of city depositories. Public libraries, and even some community college libraries, are in a position to make improved bibliographic control a reality. These libraries should be encouraged to do so by librarians, state libraries, and by organizations such as the American Library Association's Government Documents Round Table.

CATALOGING AND CLASSIFICATION

The notion that local documents collections in public libraries are provided with little in the way of cataloging and classification is still questionable and needs further research. In her 1976 questionnaire and telephone survey, Deborah Babel found that thirteen out of fifteen public libraries that responded, or 86 percent, classified their local government documents. The most common classification used was the Dewey Decimal Classification, used by ten, or 67 percent, of the responding libraries. Library of Congress Classification was used by 6 percent of the public libraries responding. Of the fourteen university libraries that responded, the Dewey Decimal Classification was used by three, or 21 percent, while two (14 percent) used the Library of Congress Classification. A majority of six university libraries, or 43 percent, did not classify their local documents.[28] Again, it must be stressed that these figures are subject to question, as only twenty-nine of the fifty-one libraries surveyed provided a response, giving the survey a response rate of 57 percent. It is, however, the only survey in existence as of this date that measures the classification, cataloging, reference service, and archival retention of local government documents on a nationwide basis. This is obviously another area that needs further inquiry.

As for cataloging, Babel found that 73 percent of the public libraries responding, and 93 percent of the university libraries responding, provided some cataloging. Of the 73 percent of public libraries providing cataloging, 60 percent provided full cataloging of documents, and 13 percent gave partial cataloging. Subject access to local documents was reported by 100 percent of the public libraries that responded. This high percentage appeared to be a result of the fact that at least 73 percent of the public libraries relied on their technical services department for processing. The high overall subject access may also be related to the use of vertical files in eight (53 percent) of the public libraries, although this is an assumption to be drawn from the data, rather than a valid conclusion. University libraries that responded seemed to provide better cataloging in terms of percentages. Nine of the fourteen university libraries (64 percent) provided full cataloging, while four (29 percent) provided partial cataloging. The university libraries depended more on *Library of Congress Subject Headings* (LCSH) for subject access. Eleven of the university libraries (79 percent) used LCSH for their local documents. This was contrasted with the public libraries, of which 53 percent used LCSH, while another 33 percent used *Sears List of Subject Headings.*[29]

As far as the actual catalog entries are concerned, standard practice usually has given main entry to the corporate author.[30] The second edition of the *Anglo-American Cataloging Rules* (AACR2) has modified this practice. Bernardine Hoduski, a member of the American Library Association's Government Documents Round Table, in a critique of the draft of AACR2, saw problems with entry of government documents. AACR2, she pointed out, makes fewer entries under corporate author and more entries under personal author and title than did AACR1.[31] This would result in more cataloging work for documents librarians, who, according to Hoduski, prefer corporate author entry. As well documented as Hoduski's stand is, one can only agree with her on the point that AACR2 means additional cataloging work. Librarians still have authority under AACR2 Rule 21.1B2 to make entries under corporate author, provided certain conditions exist. Rule 21.1B3 provides for added entries under named corporate bodies. Therefore, AACR2's provision for main entry under title or personal author does not necessarily signal the end of entries under corporate author. In fact, Elaine Svenonius, a faculty member at the University of California, Los Angeles, Graduate School of Library and Information Science, has written that it may not be necessary to use corporate author entries as a means of tying together in one place in the card catalog all the publications of a specific government agency. There may be other, more important ways of linking documents together, such as part-whole relationships.[32] Series added entries, for example, would be one way to provide the necessary part-whole links.

PUBLICITY FOR THE COLLECTION

Librarians often find that some promotion of the local government documents collection is necessary. This is sometimes a result of poor cataloging practices. Separate collection policies, too, often keep the collections hidden from the public's eye. A lack of knowledge among library users that a collection of local documents is part of the library's collection is often incorrectly interpreted by librarians as a lack of interest in them. Yuri Nakata wrote of publicity problems:

One of the most frequently cited reasons, in a questionnaire sent to Chicago area libraries, for not collecting local documents was lack of user interest. It has been demonstrated in these same libraries that once users became aware of the documents collection and its information potential, interest increases dramatically.[33]

Nakata then went on to list ways of giving the documents some publicity, such as displays and exhibits, posters and bulletin boards, bibliographies, tours, bookmarks, browsing areas, acquisition lists, special programs, newsletters, newspapers, lectures, and user instruction. Deborah Hunt also has offered a number of publicity suggestions, including television news coverage and outreach programs.[34]

In discussing Marguerite Murrell's 1950 thesis on documents use, Peter Hernon extracted two points from the study that would help increase awareness of the local documents collection. One point is a consideration of the audience for whom the publicity is intended, and the second is educating the library staff about the information value of the documents.[35] Footnote 70 of Hernon's article is a lengthy bibliography of articles concerning documents publicity. The citations in Hernon's article relate to publicity for federal and state documents, but presumably have applications that might be adopted for local documents.

In Denmark, Ingerlise Koefoed, Library Inspector for State Inspection of Public Libraries, Copenhagen, has reported that the Lyngby-Taarbaek Municipal Library took one of its local information exhibits to a major shopping center, where questions about information activities were answered by a staff of librarians.[36]

The watchword, then, is imagination.

REFERENCE SERVICE

If one accepts the figures presented in the previously mentioned surveys of William C. Robinson and Deborah Babel, it can be said that most libraries that collect local government documents are aware of the value of local documents reference service and attempt to provide it in various forms. In his survey of Tennessee libraries, Robinson found that 91 percent of the sixty-seven libraries responding to his questionnaire provided reference service to users of local documents.[37] Babel measured reference service by what she defined as "information service," an amalgam of services ranging from documents available for circulation, to the availability of photocopying facilities. Among these information services were two categories entitled "formal instruction" and "informal instruction." In terms of formal instruction, only one responding public library, or 6 percent of the total respondents, provided formal instruction in the use of local documents. Measurement of informal instruction was more encouraging, as seven public libraries, or 47 percent of the respondents, saw fit to provide it.

Babel reported that 36 percent of responding university libraries provided formal instruction, while 79 percent provided informal instruction. Since the university library figures add up to over 100 percent, it would appear that there might be a small statistical error involved, or else there was some overlap between the libraries in both categories.[38] Although Robinson's and Babel's percentages are not within a few percentage points of each other, their results are on the higher end of the scale, which might have some validity with regard to the amount of reference service actually provided.

Yuri Nakata devoted a chapter to reference service in *Organizing a Local Government Documents Collection*. She wrote, "Because of the lack of good bibliographic control of local documents, the quality of the reference service provided for these materials is dependent almost entirely on the ability of the reference librarian."[39]

She is right. The reference librarian who is not familiar with the scope, form, and content of the documents in a collection will have difficulty extracting the information contained therein, unless some form of subject index is maintained. Otherwise, the librarian must rely on the documents of the agency most likely to produce the information being requested, along with any indication that the title of the document might give as to its contents. Of course, neither agency nor title are 100 percent indicative of a document's content. Cheryl Winter Lewy, of the Chicago Municipal Reference Library, has pointed out that the emphasis ". . . on form rather than substance in most attempts to list and index the available material . . ." has contributed to the confusion in the use of local documents.[40]

Problems with reference service might, in fact, influence the organization and indexing of the collection, so that its arrangement might be responsive to the more common types of reference questions. A survey by the reference librarians could determine the nature of requests by users. For example, if most requests were for specific documents, either by agency name or title, it might benefit reference service to select a library classification scheme that organized the documents by agency or alphabetically by title, or one that achieved a combination of those two features. Such schemes might be supplemented by a ready reference card index, solely for information extracted from the content of the documents.

On the other hand, if most reference requests were of a subject nature, the librarian might elect to arrange the documents by a classification scheme that used a subject grouping. Documents issued by one agency might then be scattered through the collection, but their titles could be gathered together in a card catalog under a corporate author added entry.

It is up to the librarian to determine which type of arrangement would perform best in any particular library, depending upon the types of questions received. For example, Benjamin Shearer, Librarian at East Tennessee State University, writing about reference service and statistical information contained in local documents, said, "The fact is that most statistical questions are asked by subject, not by main entry, title, or office or [*sic*] origin.''[41]

Shearer offered no factual evidence to support his written statement, and whether it applied to questions beyond those which are statistical was not clear. This is another area suitable for further research.

In summary, it is fair to say that those libraries that collect local documents use them as reference tools to varying degrees. Bernard M. Fry, Dean of the Graduate Library School at Indiana University, hopes that those libraries that do not make as much use of them as they should will eventually bring them into the "mainstream" of reference service.[42]

ARCHIVAL RETENTION

The library that collects local government documents must sooner or later determine which documents are to be retained and how long the retention period should be. Since most of these documents contain information that will some day interest local historians, their historical value must be considered along with their reference utility as criteria in determining their retention.

A library that acquires depository status may wish, at that time, to determine the retention period of documents to be collected, as well as any restrictions on the types of documents to be acquired. There are at least three archival retention options:

1. The library becomes the central repository for all local documents;
2. If the municipality or town has a local archives, the library may turn over to the archivist any documents it has held for a specified length of time;
3. The library may enter into cooperative arrangements with nearby libraries, a local or regional archive, or an historical society. Such arrangements would designate length of retention, subject emphasis for each participant, disposing of duplicate documents, and whether the archives would be centrally located or dispersed among the members.

In terms of the first option, evidence suggests that libraries that do collect local documents are also serving as archivists for them. Yuri Nakata reported in the Illinois Local Documents Project's Final Report that in a field of eighty-three libraries surveyed, fifty-eight of the responding libraries had collections dating to 1950, and seventy-three libraries had collections dating to 1900.[43] Babel's survey found that five out of thirteen responding public libraries, or 38 percent, had collected local documents for more than sixty years.[44] In Robinson's survey of Tennessee libraries' local documents collections, no figures were reported, as most of the libraries could not supply archival information.

In any event, the library will want to assist development of its archival retention policy by surveying other collections in the area, such as those at City Hall, the city archives, the local historical society, and other area libraries. Frederick M. Miller, in writing about urban historical documentation, has stated with respect to forming archival collections:

The initial stages in the development of an urban archives typically involve surveys and bibliographic research. The geographical area of interest must be defined, its history intensively studied and current research activities investigated. The holdings of existing repositories are reveiwed. The first major project will often be a records survey, an examination of collections which are not yet housed in any archives. As a result of these activities, a picture of the potential collecting policy and the area's research needs will emerge. At the same time there will be active consultations with government, academic and community groups. The administrative arrangements of the archives will also be an important early consideration. Most urban archives are units of other libraries, either public or university. This can cause serious difficulties, since the needs and interests of the archives can easily be perceived as being peripheral to the mission of the institution.[45]

In addition to the factors Miller mentioned, an additional consideration may be the cost-benefits. Maintenance costs may be high, even prohibitive for a library without adequate financial resources. If this is the case, the library might find a cooperative archival arrangement fiscally expedient. There are, however, opposing arguments to such cooperative arrangements. Philadelphia, for example, has established a cooperative Urban Archives, drawing upon the wealth of material in public and private libraries and institutions in the area. Yet, according to Miller, the project suffers from a lack of coordination.[46] The Houston Metropolitan Research Center, another attempt at a cooperative urban archives, ran into financial difficulties, and turned its operations over completely to the Houston Public Library. This turned out to be an advantage for the archives, as it developed its own identity within the library and was free from the institutional rivalries that had disrupted the cooperative arrangement. Other problems with cooperative arrangements include establishing subject specialties, and deciding how gifts from donors will be equitably distributed.[47]

In speaking of the roles of libraries and archives, Bernard M. Fry has written:

The "primary responsibilities of archives are in the area of records administration rather than research assistance" although in the recent past new concepts of greater access to records have broadened this viewpoint. In contrast, libraries emphasize a wide range of information services, including open stacks for browsing, and provide effective reference service, indexing tools, access to data banks, and document delivery.

Libraries and archives represent related and essential public service functions and should be viewed as complementary, not competitive. The last decade of liberalization of archival access and use underscores this point. The development of computer-based centralized technical processing, together with on-line capabilities via national networks, make close cooperation imperative between libraries and archives in their mutually reinforcing services to the public.[48]

Some of the features that Fry suggests have come into being in the form of BRISC, the acronym for the Baltimore Region Institutional Studies Center. The center is primarily concerned with institutional research by academics, but it also serves the agencies and organizations that deposited the records, as well as the general public. BRISC houses different collections, ranging from private papers to agency and organization records.[49] BRISC has indexed all documents at the file unit level, employing the descriptors listed in the *Urban Information Thesaurus*, and has input the information into a computer system data base called ARCHON.[50] ARCHON (ARCHives ON-line) allows searching by means of either a subject index printout, or on-line searching of records by subject, geographic location, and date.[51] The *Urban Information Thesaurus* also offers the opportunity for a computer application of a library's local documents collection. Computer indexing of local documents is discussed in more detail in a later chapter in this book.

As can be seen from the foregoing, cooperation is probably the most important factor in successful preservation of local materials so that they have a high utility. This is true whether the arrangement is a regional center such as BRISC, a public library as in Houston, or a network affiliation of units, such as in Philadelphia.

SEPARATE VERSUS INTEGRATED COLLECTIONS

It almost goes without saying that the classification scheme a library chooses for its local documents collection might be influenced by whether the collection was integrated with the general collection or kept in a separate area.

An integrated collection might logically employ whatever classification scheme was used for the general collection, thereby reducing library patron confusion and simplifying the processing of documents. A separate collection, to which only librarians have access, might use whatever classification scheme the librarians find has the greatest utility.

In Robinson's survey of Tennessee libraries, 55 percent of responding public libraries reported having separate collections of local government documents. Academic libraries leaned in the other direction, with 80 percent reporting integrated collections. By contrast, Deborah Babel found that 67 percent of public libraries combined local documents and local history materials into one separate collection. Twenty-nine percent of university libraries surveyed by Babel integrated local documents into the general collection, while 50 percent integrated local documents into a separate documents collection of publications from many levels of government, and from many governments. Robinson did not distinguish between integrated documents collections and integrated general collections on this point, so his 80 percent figure may be too high, reflecting the lack of a more detailed categorization, such as the one Babel used.[52]

Of course, there are other factors that lead to a decision for or against a separate collection. The size of the local documents collections, the availability of bibliographies or checklists, as well as time and money should be considered. Peter Hernon, Michael Waldo, Susan Berman, Mary Jane Hilburger, and Yuri Nakata have all discussed advantages and disadvantages of separate collections for local government documents. Their discussions should be consulted for an in-depth look at this issue, as it is one that has persisted a long time without definite resolution.[53]

LOCAL GOVERNMENT INFORMATION STORED IN COMPUTER DATA BASES

As more communities move toward new methods of information management and automated record keeping, librarians may find that certain local information is not available in printed form. Electronic storage of data has arrived in local government operations. As a result, information sometimes appears in printed form only upon the request of city officials, or in accordance with law at the end of the legally established reporting period or fiscal year.

There are no clear pathways yet for libraries faced with obtaining electronically stored information. Maintaining good working relations with city government officials would seem one of the best ways of obtaining needed information. Michael Shannon has asked, however, whether a computer data base can be considered a local document, and whether a computer printout has the same status as a published document.[54]

The New York Municipal Reference and Research Center maintains a public computer terminal with access to the city's Integrated Financial Management System data base. Information can be located and produced in hard copy on a computer printout. Michael Shannon has asked, however, whether a computer data base can be considered a local document, and whether a computer printout has the same status as a published document.[54]

It probably will be necessary to look to the American Library Association, state legislatures, and the judicial system for guidelines in this evolving area of documentation.

2

Evaluation of Local Government Documents Classification Schemes

In the selection of a classification scheme for the organization of a library's local government documents, there are two considerations that should be taken into account first, since they will define in large part the foundation upon which other, subsequent choices may be made. The first of these considerations is the type of use normally made of the collection by library users and staff. The second consideration is whether any one scheme under scrutiny for use with the collection has been designed with particular features, which, when applied, will meet certain specific objectives in regard to shelf arrangement, ease of processing, method of access, and so forth. Having as close a match as possible between these two foci is a wise decision, which will mitigate any potential conflicts between document use and access.

A statistical survey of the use made of local documents by both librarians and library users will help to define the role of local government documents as sources of information. For example, are most approaches to the documents by title, agency, personal author, corporate author, or subject? A weight in one direction or another might suggest the difference between choosing a subject classification arrangement or an alphabetical arrangement by title. If a specific agency's documents are in demand, an arrangement which brings together all the publications of each city agency might be more practical.

Whether the local documents collection is separate or integrated into the main collection will have a definite influence on the scheme selected. For documents which are integrated into the general collection, the library would normally want to use the same scheme as is used for the general collection to keep processing costs down and library users' confusion to a minimum.

On the other hand, if the collection is separate from the general collection and not directly accessible to library users without going through a member of the staff, then the use of a specialized classification scheme would not necessarily cause any confusion among users, while the library would gain the benefits of any scheme considered superior to that used for the general collection.

Whether or not computer searching capabilities are available also may influence the choice. Some newer schemes are designed with computer access in mind, while some of the older general classification schemes are thought to have some adaptability for use with computers.

The size of the collection is also a factor not to be overlooked. A very small collection might not warrent a formal classification scheme. An accession number arrangement might be a more practical approach for a small collection, as well as a collection which has excellent card catalog access or has been computer coded.

Once access to the documents is provided by selection of an appropriate classification scheme, the next step should be improved access to the information contained in the documents. Unless good subject cataloging is part of the processing agenda for local government documents, access to content information will be poor without some subject indexing. As many local documents do not contain tables of contents or indexes, a certain amount of indexing is a good way to enhance the retrieval power of the classification scheme and descriptive cataloging. The final chapter of this book is a survey of three indexing systems that may be used with a local government documents collection.

What follows in this chapter is a scheme-by-scheme enumeration; any of these schemes may be used to classify local government documents. Some are general bibliographic schemes, some are tailored for special collections, and others are solely for government documents. They have been divided into three major categories, the first of which contains those schemes which allow subject arrangements of documents. This group includes the Dewey Decimal and Library of Congress Classifications, two of the most widely used schemes in the United States. The second category, which is by far the largest, contains those schemes that provide archival arrangements by issuing agency. While this type of arrangement has a certain predictability, there are certainly many variations on the theme. In the last category is a scheme which has computer applicability.

Chart 1 provides a basic comparison of characteristics common to the seventeen classification schemes discussed thereafter. The chart is not intended to be complete in scope and depth, but rather to serve as a general guide, particularly to some of the lesser-known schemes. The column on the far right lists the pages on which begin discussions of each scheme.

SUBJECT ARRANGEMENTS

Melvil Dewey, *Dewey Decimal Classification and Relative Index*, Edition 19, edited under the direction of Benjamin A. Custer, 3 vols. (Albany, N.Y.: Forest Press, 1979).

Chart 1
Comparison of Selected Features of Seventeen Classification Schemes

Classification Schemes

Name of Classification Scheme and Year of Publication	Document Arrangements			Use with following types of documents									Status of Collection		See Page
	S (Subject)	A (Archival)	C (Computr)	L	S	C	R	N	T	F	I	N	I (Integrated)	S (Separate)	
DDC, 1894, 19th ed., 1976	X			X	X	X	X	X	X	X	X	X	X	X	20
LC, early 1900's	X			X	X	X	X	X	X	X	X	X	X	X	25
Glidden, 1942	X			X	X	X	X	X	X	X	X	X		X	27
Harvard, 1913, revised, 1973	X			X	X	X	X	X	X				X*	X	34
NYCP&HL, 1963	X			X	X	X	X	X						X	41
Wisconsin, 1932	X			X		X								X	45
NLC/USCM, 1970	X			X	X		X							X	47
Swank, 1940		X		X	X	X		X						X	52
Jackson, 1941		X		X	X	X	X	X	X	X	X			X	57
U Dayton, 1979		X		X		X					X			X	62
U Nebraska, 1973		X		X							X			X	67
Plain "J", 1972		X		X	X	X	X	X	X	X	X	X	X*	X	72
Rochester, NY PL, 1939		X		X		X					X			X	78
U Makerere, 1962		X		X	X	X	X	X	X	X	X	X		X	82
Albany, 1973		X		X	X	X	X		X					X*	86
U El Paso, 1976		X		X	X	X		X				X	X	X	91
CODOC, 1974		X	X+	X	X	X	X	X	X	X	X	X		X	95

*Integrated use only with Library of Congress Classification.
+Provides archival shelf arrangement, and uses computer coding.

The *Dewey Decimal Classification* (DDC) provides an arrangement of materials by subject, according to discipline. The subject approach of the DDC, together with its virtually unlimited subject range, makes it an appropriate scheme to use for the classification of government documents from all levels of government.

If the normal subject classification approach of the DDC is followed, there will be subject scatter of documents throughout the general collection, provided, of course, that the documents are integrated into the general collection. As to the likelihood of a library employing an integrated approach to the organization of local documents, Robinson's survey of Tennessee libraries indicated that separate collections were preferred by 55 percent of public libraries. Deborah Babel's survey discovered only 6 percent of public libraries and 29 percent of university libraries integrated their local documents with the general collection. Meanwhile, Yuri Nakata's survey of Illinois libraries found that 91 percent of the libraries surveyed had local documents collections numbering less than 500 volumes. If these approximations are correct, the typical collection of local government documents would be a separate collection, under 500 volumes. Consequently, subject scatter when using the DDC would be limited in terms of dispersion in physical distance, since all documents would be located within a relatively small shelf area.[55]

There is, however, an alternative to this subject arrangement which is recognized by the Dewey Office but does not have official approval. The alternative is known as classification by attraction and is described in Section 13.33 of the Editor's Introduction to the nineteenth edition of the *Dewey Decimal Classification*:

Because of special local interest or special collections of books, it may on occasion appear desirable to bring together all works on a given subject in only one of the several possible disciplines, e.g., *all* works on Jews in 296, *all* works on automobiles, in 629.2.

An extension of this practice is the complete reversal of DDC order. For example, a library devoted to travel and area study, or to maps, might make an administrative decision to arrange its collections entirely by place. To achieve this arrangement it could use the "Areas" notations for the basic classes, followed, when appropriate, by 0 and the DDC subject numbers. Then everything on Japan would be placed in class 52; religion in 5202; economic situation in 52033, art in 5207. In such a system, works not limited by area could be placed in notation 0 followed by the regular DDC notation, e.g., economic conditions of the whole world 033. Needless to say, this kind of use of DDC would be purely local, and would receive no support from central classification services.[56]

Therefore, a library that wished to do so could classify all its local government documents in class 352, and add a subject notation, thereby bringing together in one place on its shelves all its local documents in a microcosmic subject arrangement within the class as a whole. Obviously, this would serve to minimize any subject scattering of local government documents throughout the classes of the DDC. Still a third way of treating local documents would be possible under the DDC, by classing items under the appropriate Area Tables notation.

Yuri Nakata has drawn attention to a method of classification for a separate collection whereby the local documents are classed by subject, using the DDC in normal fashion. Above the DDC class number, a geographic location tag is added, such as Ill. for an Illinois document, or Chi. for a City of Chicago document. The geographical location tag, above the DDC class number, would be of the same ilk as the commonly used R, which is normally employed to indicate reference works. The location tag would have the same effect, that is, creating and identifying a special collection of local documents.[57]

Location tags will serve the small collection well, as they will provide not just a separate collection, but a focus on that collection. Furthermore, since the tags would be used in conjunction with the DDC number, integration of documents into the general collection is an option that always remains open. As the size and diversity of the local documents collection increases, however, libraries considering use of location tags will also have to look at patterns of use, ease of filing and retrieval, and the necessary additional processing work, before coming to any decision.

With or without location tags, when using the DDC, a preference for either an integrated or separate arrangement might depend on the size of the collection, the policy as to whether or not documents are allowed to circulate, and any data the library has obtained relative to patterns of document use. In an integrated collection, library users might prefer to have all local documents in one part of the general collection for easy browsing, such as in class 352, Municipal Government. In the event the collection is large, perhaps in the range of one thousand to two thousand items, then this type of arrangement might decrease the ability to retrieve a document, particularly if the class numbers were not carried far enough to achieve specificity. The library would have to Cutter the documents by title or agency, or add an accession number, to decrease any confusion within the collection. The alternative is to use the standard DDC subject approach and tolerate the subject scatter.

In addition to all the factors discussed thus far, the popularity of the DDC also might be taken into account when selecting a classification scheme for local government publications. Since most of the public libraries in the United States still use the DDC, the choice of a classification that is compatible with that used for the library's general collection makes sense in terms of familiarity with library users. It has cost-benefit implications also. Processing could be performed by the technical services department, along with other accessions.

For libraries that have computer systems available, there are also the possible computer applications of the DDC to consider. Gordon Stevenson,

Associate Professor at the School of Library and Information Science, State University of New York, Albany, has suggested, "Looking to the future, DDC has the capability of developing into a system that can exploit some of the potentials of the computer and at the same time provide a system of class numbers for shelving materials."[58]

Stevenson did not go on to explain what he meant by the exploitation of the computer. Presumably, he was implying that since the DDC uses a numeric hierarchy, the facility with which computers manipulate numbers could be applied to the ability of the DDC's notation to express an array of concepts within classes and class subdivisions, and do so with increasing specificity. The ability of the DDC's notation to be associated with the taxonomic structure of the classification, as opposed to the often oblique structure of the *Library of Congress Classification* notation, was something else Stevenson left unsaid, as was the increasing number of synthetic elements being incorporated into DDC revisions that might someday allow computer searching in a Boolean fashion. In fact, Arnold S. Wajenberg, Principal Cataloger at the University of Illinois at Champaign-Urbana, recently published a proposal for incorporating subject coding of DDC call numbers in the Library of Congress's MARC record.[59] The advantages of searching on facets of a classification number vis-à-vis some other method, such as a list of subject headings or index terms, will most likely prove its value as on-line searching becomes more common. These are still just opinions though, not a manifesto that the DDC is better suited to a computer environment than any other classification scheme.

It is also true that the Library of Congress's MARC record provides a descriptive field for the DDC classification number and that DDC numbers are provided as part of the Library of Congress's Cataloging-in-Publication (CIP) program. Although these two provisions are important features in an on-line copy cataloging situation, they seem of negligible use in the processing of local government documents, since local documents almost always require original cataloging. Therefore, if computer compatibility of any classification scheme is a prime consideration of the library, then equal consideration must also be given to the University of Guelph's CODOC System, which will be discussed later in this chapter.

From an economic standpoint, the choice of a classification scheme which is apt to survive indefinitely might also enter into a decision process. Elaine Svenonius, a faculty member at UCLA's Graduate School of Library and Information Science, recently suggested that the DDC is better suited for survival than other widely used schemes, such as the *Library of Congress Classification*, because the DDC conforms to international standards, and provides more synthetic capabilities with each revision, while, ". . . LC continues in its enumerative mode."[60] Through constant revision, the DDC is less likely to lose its hospitality for new subjects and its specificity of call numbers. Other features that help to ensure its longevity are predictability in application of principles and its multipurpose library application.

Library of Congress, *Classification: Class J, Political Science,* 2nd ed. (Washington, D.C.: Library of Congress, 1924; reprinted, 1956).

The *Library of Congress Classification* (LC Classification) also offers a subject arrangement of materials. LC Classification applies the principle of literary warrant to its subject class arrangements, and the result is that, like the DDC, there is a scattering of materials by subject, and sometimes also by the manner in which the author treated the subject matter. For example, in Class JS, which is a subdivision of Political Science Class J, there are provisions for local executive annual reports and municipal codes. Documents from municipal health, welfare, social, and regulatory agencies would be located in other classes, and therefore would be scattered throughout the collection, provided that the local documents were integrated with the general collection. Likewise, city planning commission documents would be located in Class NA, Fine Arts, while any economic development reports would be located in Class H, Social Sciences.

The disadvantages to such subject scatter will, once again, be related to patterns of use of the local documents, the sizes of both the general and local documents collections, as well as whether the documents are separate or part of an integrated collection.

For libraries that collect local documents from a number of cities, towns, and states, there may be varying amounts of geographical scatter, because LC Classification does not provide uniform geographical subdivisions throughout the scheme, whereas the DDC does. For example, annual reports of United States mayors may be classed alphabetically by city in Class JS 13. With local city ordinances, however, there exist the options of arrangement by region, alphabetically by state, or alphabetically by city.

LC Classification does provide for documents acquired from foreign nations and all other levels of government, as does the DDC. This is an important feature in using a general bibliographic scheme specifically in conjunction with the acquisition of foreign government documents. Other classifications, particulary the more specialized schemes, do not always provide for foreign materials. For those libraries that collect foreign local documents, there is the additional benefit of shared cataloging when using the LC Classification, but only if the Library of Congress acquired and cataloged the same foreign documents.

As far as shared cataloging of local documents from cities in the United States is concerned, unless the library in question is located in one of the fourteen principal cities from which the Library of Congress collects local documents, then that library must do its own original cataloging. The fourteen cities from which local documents are collected by the Library of Congress are: New York; Los Angeles; Washington, D.C.; Alexandria, Virginia; Falls Church, Virginia; Baltimore; Atlanta; Boston; Chicago; Detroit; Houston; St. Paul; St. Louis; and Dallas. There are exceptions, however, as in recent years the Library of Congress has acquired selected local documents from a wider range of communities. In most cases, these documents are in some way connected with local use of federal funds.

In terms of notation, LC Classification has the advantage of a high degree of specificity, a plus for those libraries with large, diverse collections of local documents. Unfortunately, because of complexities of deriving the notation through LC Classification's general and special subclasses, and its many vertical tables, the notation often is not expressive of the subject matter, nor even of the subject arrangement hierarchy, since in the latter instance, the Library of Congress sometimes employs hierarchies tailored to fit its own collection, rather than using some evolutionary descending format. Therefore, a library with a large separate local documents collection might want the notation and shelf arrangement to display a schematic structural organization and might find this difficult to do with the LC Classification.

There have been varying opinions on the LC Classification's notational structure, particularly in relation to an automated library setting. Gordon Stevenson has written that:

Not only has an inefficient and illogical system of subject headings been perpetuated on the MARC tapes, but each year thousands of titles are entered into this system tagged with LC class numbers which are almost completely useless in providing subject access through a computerized classified catalog. At the same time, in order to take advantage of the economic savings to be derived from networks and centralization, hundreds of libraries are switching from a system which shows some real potential for new modes of classified bibliographical access to a system with a nonhierarchical notation which is hopelessly antiquated for computerized retrieval systems.[61]

Stevenson did not address the question of the importance, if any, attached to computer subject searching through notational devices, particularly since microfiche listings of LC's subject headings are easily available to would-be searchers of data base entries tagged with those so-called inefficient and illogical subject headings. Granted, inconsistencies do exist in the *Library of Congress Subject Headings*. There has been an attempt, however, to arrange the *Library of Congress Subject Headings* and LC Classification's notation in an alphabetical systematic order. Further attempts along these lines should help to ease the difficulties of using the notational devices, and even the subject headings, in classified form for computer subject retrieval.[62]

In a countervailing view, Elaine Svenonius has suggested, "Because LC, for the most part, is not arranged logically or hierarchically, it might be better suited to an automated environment."[63]

One assumes that Svenonius has alluded here to the idea that the computer application of the LC Classification has made shelf location and subclass hierarchy less important because of the speed with which computers can locate, or "hit," items in random sequence. This implies that in such a situation, it might be better to have a distinctive computer "address" for information at the file level in the data base. LC Classification's unique notational symbols might provide the distinctive addresses needed.

Overall, LC Classification, when used for a local government documents collection, does not fare much better or worse than the DDC.

In addition to the preferences previously mentioned concerning subject scatter, notation, and computer application, a library's choice of LC Classification over any alternates for use with a documents collection should also weigh the importance of consistent classification practices throughout the library, user familiarity with call numbers and locations, as well as the size and diversity of the collection, use patterns, and whether integrated or separate.

Sophia H. Glidden and D. G. Marchus, *Library Classification for Public Administration Materials* (Chicago: American Library Association, 1942).

Glidden and Marchus's scheme offers a classified subject arrangement for a separate collection of public administration materials and easily accommodates local government documents as subsets of those materials. This scheme is based in part on a 1928 scheme for political science collections, authored by William Anderson and Sophia Glidden. Anderson was Director of the Bureau for Research in Government at the University of Minnesota, and Glidden was a librarian at the bureau.[64]

According to Deborah Babel's paper in 1976, the Glidden and Marchus public administration classification was still being used by the Bureau of the Census's Social and Economic Statistics Administration (SESA) Library.[65] Upon recent inquiry, the library, which is now known as the Census Bureau Library, has for the past several years been converting from the Glidden and Marchus scheme to the LC Classification. No doubt the inclusion of Library of Congress call numbers and subject headings in the Superintendent of Documents' *Monthly Catalog* during this same time period had some bearing on the reported conversion.

In preparing the classification, Glidden visited a number of libraries in the field of public administration and spoke to librarians, gathering their suggestions, comments, and needs for a classification scheme. Her investigation led to the development of a scheme that has the primary features of a flexible, expansive notation, subject schedules that display subject relationships, and a combined subject headings list and index.[66] In addition to local government documents, which are designated as municipal or metropolitan by the scheme, the schedules also allow for classification of those documents produced by federal, state, county, regional, territorial, and foreign governments, as well as those produced by nongovernmental (private) agencies.

The subclasses of each class are usually arranged with general materials first, followed by categories in descending order, either by relative importance or by level of government. For example, Class J, Planning, begins with a subdivision for planning procedures, that has been given the class name Technical Procedure. The Technical Procedure subclass is followed by Resources Planning. Levels of governmental planning follow, and these subclasses are arranged hierarchically: National Planning, Regional Planning, State Planning, County Planning, and City Planning.

Even where a seemingly obvious descending order is possible, it is not always used. For example, in Class X, Public Works, there are the following subdivisions of subclass X 61, Classes of Roads:

X 61	Classes of Roads
611	Trunk Highways, Arterial Streets, Freeways
612	By-pass and belt line roads
613	Secondary and feeder roads
616	Cul-de-sacs
617	Alleys
618	Parkways, Boulevards

In this instance, Parkways and Boulevards have been grouped together because they usually are landscaped, while subclasses 611 through 617 are not. Another example of selective subordering is in the subdivisions of Class X 212, the Construction of Institutions:

X 212	Institutions
2122	Religious buildings
2123	Health institutions
2125	Educational institutions
2129	Penal and correctional institutions

Other than putting the pious first and the sinners last, this subarrangement has no obvious logic other than alluding to some utopian order of social significance. An alphabetical arrangement might have been more useful. Alphabetical arrangements seem to be least preferred in this classification if some other order or progression is available, whether obvious or obscure.

Glidden and Marchus have provided a liberal supply of scope notes at all class and subclass levels. The scope notes are brief, but are an admirable, positive feature of the scheme that allows ranking of the Glidden and Marchus classification as close in overall development and sophistication to the DDC and LC schemes. "See" and "See also" notes are also in great abundance.

The Subject Index to the Glidden and Marchus classification, upon examination, is similar to the DDC's *Relative Index*. Also designed for use as a subject headings list, Glidden and Marchus have listed subjects alphabetically, followed by the class number. If the subject heading chosen for use by the librarian is not used in the Subject Index, there is a "See" reference to the appropriate preferred heading. "See also" references provide guidance to other potential subject headings, plus the suggested headings' class numbers. In a separate column to the right of some subject headings, there is a list of "See" and "See also" card catalog references, which is a plus for any library electing to use the scheme's subject headings in its card catalog. The references, typically, are mostly lateral or downward in the hierarchy. Of course, whether or not these subject headings are used will depend upon cataloging practices in the library and whether cards for local documents will appear in the main card catalog. If the main card catalog uses subject headings not compatible with those used by Glidden and Marchus, the result will be added work by the catalogers to resolve any conflicts.

Glidden and Marchus have selected a natural-language, controlled vocabulary for their subject headings. The subject headings are derivatives or modifications of subject headings that were being used in 1942 by the Public Affairs Information Service and the Library of Congress.[67] The headings consist normally of one or two words, a noun, or an adjective plus noun. Examples are: Achievement tests, Administrative areas, Administrative assistants, Administrative courts, Advisory councils, Benefit societies, Managers, Personnel, Youth hostels, Zoological gardens, and Social problems. There are some exceptions to the adjective plus noun and single noun forms. These are evident in the use of verb-subject headings such as Labelling and Yachting. Some gerundives are used, such as Mapping, Aerial, and Bill drafting, although this type of use tends to preserve the adjective plus noun form. Additionally, varying types of phrase subject headings are used, of which Demonstration work in Agriculture, and Leaves of Absence are examples. Most headings on the list have no subdivisions, and of those that do, one subdivision is the maximum. Of course, in actual catalog use, there is a potential for two, or, in some instances, three subdivisions, as place and form subdivisions are authorized in two auxiliary tables to the classification.

The adjective and noun form, used so frequently by Glidden and Marchus, has a collocating effect in the card catalog, bringing together various aspects of a subject. The authors have enhanced this feature in some instances by inverting terms, as exemplified in Zoning, County, and Zoning, Urban.

Table 1 sets forth the mnemonics and general outline of the classification.

Tables 2 and 3 set forth the Form Letters and Form Subdivisions, the Form Letters being employed when the collection contains documents from several levels of government.

As can be seen from Tables 1, 2, and 3, the scheme combines the mnemonic similarities of the LC Classification with numeric subdivisions, the latter having been applied according to principles of the DDC.[68]

Table 1.
Glidden and Marchus, Classification for Public Administration Materials—Outline of Classes

A	General Reference
B	Society The State Government
C	Constitutional History and Law
D	International Relations
F	Citizen Participation in Government Politics Elections
G	The Legislature Law
H	The Judiciary Courts Legal Profession
I	The Executive Public Administration Administrative Law
J	Planning Zoning
K	Personnel Administration
L	Public Finance
N	National Defense Law Enforcement Police Fire Protection Safety
O	Health Medical Profession Sanitation
OA	Recreation Commercialized Amusements Clubs
P	Education Libraries
Q	Welfare Dependency Social Insurance Crime
R	Labor
T	Economics Industry Business Finance Standardization
U	Government and Business Public Enterprise
V	Public Utilities
W	Transportation Traffic Communication
X	Public Works
XA	Housing
Y	Natural Resources
Z	Agriculture

The Classes E, M, and S have been left open for expansion, and double-letter combinations may also be used if more classes need to be added at some later date. For a separate collection of perhaps one thousand or fewer documents, the classes provided should be adequate without using the expansion features.

Like some of the major bibliographic classifications, Glidden and Marchus's scheme begins with general reference materials. From there, the

Table 2.

Glidden and Marchus, Classification for Public Administration Materials—Form Letters

f	Federal
s	State
c	County
m	Municipal
mt	Metropolitan
r	Regional
t	Territorial
p	Private
x	Foreign

remaining subject classes follow with the law as a body of knowledge in Class C, then move in descending order to the institutions and individuals who create and enforce the law in Classes F through N, followed by agencies directly involved in social services in Classes O through Q, and ending with feet on the ground, so to speak, with classes of subjects directly affecting the natural environment, namely XA Housing, Y Natural Resources, and Z Agriculture.

The Glidden and Marchus classification was the subject of reviews in four journals in 1942. Generally, reactions were favorable, particularly for its use as a general scheme for materials in public administration libraries.

There were a few criticisms. For example, while D. J. Haykin supported its adoption in special libraries with public administration collections, he questioned whether some cost-effectiveness studies should be performed before it was adopted by public and university libraries already using the DDC or LC Classification. Haykin did admit that there were inadequate provisions for public administration materials in the DDC and LC Classification at that time, which was one of the reasons why Glidden and Marchus's scheme came into existence. Haykin also commented at the time:

The only serious criticism which can be made of the scheme as a whole is that the classes do not always follow the obvious logical sequence in the order of genetic relationship; for example, Labor precedes Economics, Planning and Zoning are sandwiched in between Administrative Law and Personnel Administration. The subordinate divisions throughout the classification are apparently limited to topics covered by the book collections of the libraries examined, without perhaps a sufficient attempt to round out the classification, say, by providing for topics which are as yet treated only in periodical literature. There is no doubt, however, that the classification is practical and will amply cover the books and pamphlets which make up today's public administration libraries.[69]

Table 3.
Glidden and Marchus, Classification for Public Administration Materials—Form Subdivisions

043	Accounting
00	Administration
042	Appropriations
09	Associations
05	Biography
044	Bounties
041	Budgets
088	Campaigns
034	Certification
025	Condemnation
096	Conferences
036	Contracts
04	Costs
001	Departmental organization
009	Departmental personnel
05	Directories
07	Equipment
088	Exhibits
045	
046	Federal aid
04	Finance
066	Forms
098	Foundations
044	Grants-in-aid
0	History
011	Inspection
005	Interdepartmental relations
003	Intergovernmental relations
077	Laboratories
038,	
039	Legal aspects
03	Legislation
034	Licenses
037	Manuals
069	Maps
034	Permits
000	Planning
02	Powers and functions
085	Publicity
06	Records
01	Regulation
06	Reporting
06	Reports

Table 3 *continued*

084	Research
036	Specifications
047	State aid
0651	Statistical methods
065	Statistics
08	Study and teaching
044	Subsidies
068	Survey methods

Haykin's comments on the uneven treatment of subjects within the various classes were an echo of Ralph R. Shaw's review several months earlier, in April 1942.[70] Shaw also added that the scheme's adoption would require much reclassification by those libraries already using the scheme published in 1928 by Anderson and Glidden.

Examples of the classification's notation, using two hypothetical local documents, are set forth in Table 4. In Table 4, two notational descriptions are provided for each document because the classification allows the geographical subdivisions to be displayed in any one of three different ways. Geographical subdivisions may be added after the form subdivison by adding a Cutter number for the state, as well as by adding LC Classification or DDC geographical subdivisions. In Table 4, the first class number in each example has been Cuttered for the state of California. The second notational example for each document has had the DDC geographical subdivision for Los Angeles County added from the DDC Area Tables. The DDC standard geographical subdivision prefix 09 has not been used in order to shorten an already lengthy notation.

Table 4.

Glidden and Marchus, Classification for Public Administration Materials—Examples of Notation

Document Description	Notation
Report on the Construction of the buildings to House the Church of Sacred Knowledge Center, in Santa Monica, California	X2122m.06C12 or X2122m.0679.493
Annual Budget of the Planning Board of Los Angeles County, California	J600c.041C12 or J600c.04179.493

In the case of the church building construction document in Table 4, it is immediately evident that neither call number is specific to the city government level. To make them so would require further Cuttering, or the addition of some other geographical symbol. The additional Cuttering would be desirable for a large local documents collection, where the grouping of documents by city would ease retrieval.

Also readily discernible from Table 4 is that the Glidden and Marchus classification's call numbers are just as long, possibly longer, than a comparable DDC or LC Classification call number. Taking the Santa Monica church building document in Table 4 as an example, it is seen to consist of the following segments:

X   Class letter. Class X is Public Works.
2   Main class number. "2" represents construction.
1   First class subdivision. "1" represents buildings.
2   Second class subdivision. "2" represents institutions.
2   Third class subdivision. "2" represents religious buildings.
m   Form letter representing a document at the municipal level of government.
.06   Form Subdivision representing a report.
C12   (or 79.493) Geographical subdivision. C12 is the Cutter number for California; 79.493 is the DDC Area Table designation for Los Angeles County.

The examples depicted in Table 4 indicate that in terms of cost-effectiveness, as well as familiarity to library users, it might be advisable for a library that uses the LC Classification or the DDC to employ those schemes for their local documents, rather than the Glidden and Marchus classification. Of course, such a decision, as previously mentioned, would have to be compatible with the needs of the library users, and with the objectives of the library in regard to the development and utilization of the local government documents collection. The Glidden and Marchus classification is still in use at the National League of Cities Municipal Reference Service in Washington, D.C.

Caroline Shillaber, *A Library Classification for City and Regional Planning* (Cambridge, Massachusetts: Harvard University Press, 1973).

Developed by the Harvard Graduate School of Design Library, *A Library Classification for City and Regional Planning* emphasizes the organization of city and regional planning documents as its title implies. This classification could be used with broader subject collections, if modifications were made to it, but would appear to work best in its present form when used with limited, separate collections of city planning materials. Most local documents will fit into this scheme. Any library that collects a significant number of publications from the mayor's office, city council, and judiciary however, is going to find this scheme inadequate without modification, since it has no provisions for documents in those categories. Some changes to little-used classes would offer one solution to such a problem, or, the mayoral, council, and court documents could be arranged in accordance with Class JS of the LC Classification, for reasons that will become evident in the course of this discussion.

If the Harvard *Library Classification for City and Regional Planning* appears familiar upon examination, there is ample reason why. It originally was devised at Harvard in 1913 by James Sturgis Pray and Theodora Kimball because no classification in existence at that time made adequate provisions for city planning materials. Harvard began instruction in city planning in 1910, the first university in the nation to do so, and needed a classification scheme that would provide for those materials. Pray and Kimball tied the scheme to Class N of the *Library of Congress Classification*. After its publication in 1913, portions of Pray and Kimball's scheme were incorporated into the LC Classification by the Library of Congress.[71] Today, it is difficult to see parallels between the Harvard scheme and the LC Classification, since Class N of the latter has gone through four revised editions and has been expanded in enormous detail. Some incorporations of the Harvard classification are more evident than others however, as is the case with LC Classification's subclass HE, Transportation and Communication, the outline of which is still markedly similar to Class 8300, et seq., of the Harvard scheme.

Pray and Kimball's original scheme was revised in 1973 by Caroline Shillaber of the same Harvard library, which is commonly known now as the Frances Loeb Library. Her revision incorporated Comey and McNamara's *State and National Planning: An Analysis of the Subject with Particular Reference to the Classification of Library Materials with Alphabetic Subject Index.*[72] As revised, the Harvard scheme now accommodates planning documents or works from the international, federal, state, county, regional, and municipal levels of government.

Shillaber's 1973 revision is divided into three parts: the class numbers and names, geographical subdivisions, and index. A very abbreviated outline of classes and class numbers is presented in Table 5.

It may not be obvious from looking at Table 5 that this scheme is highly enumerative. Like the LC Classification, many subdivisions are specific treatments of the main class, rather than a descending evolutionary hierarchy. For example, in Class 2170, "Highways, Thoroughfares, Major Streets, Urban Arterial Highways, Interurban Highways," the major subclasses are 2195, "Business Traffic"; 2205, "Pleasure Traffic"; 2220, "Local Streets"; 2230, "Special Uses"; and 2235, "Residential Streets." Additionally, some subclasses arrange documents by authorship, such as those produced by commissions, agencies, societies, and reports and studies, as well as offering subclasses for "General," "General Special," and "Special" treatments.

Since subclass numbers are specific to type and form of document, one of

Table 5.
A Library Classification for City and Regional Planning, Harvard University, Graduate School of Design—Abbreviated Outline of Classes

0	Bibliography. Periodicals. Societies.
40	Congresses, Conferences, Conventions. Exhibitions. Museums. Libraries.
200	Biography. History.
250	General Works.
500	City Planning Movement.
700	Legislation: United States.
800	Technical Procedure. Professional Practice.
900	Study and Teaching.
1200	Composition of City Plans. Planning. Replanning.
1210	Social Aspects. Economic Aspects. Esthetic Aspects.
1400	Population. Social Conditions. Man-made Environment.
	1430 Housing.
	1445 Public Health and Safety.
1500	Legal and Administrative Conditions.
1600	Organization and Subdivision of City Area by Dominant Function. Districts. Zoning.
2000	Channels of Transportation.
	2050 Streets, Roads, Footways, Highways, Vehicles.
	2350 Rapid Transit.
	2550 Waterways and Waterfronts, Commercial.
3000	Blocks and Lots. Land Subdivision. Planned Unit Development.
	4100 Parks and Reservations.
	4300 Playgrounds, Athletic Fields. Areas for Sports and Games.
	7010 County Planning.
	7030 Regional Planning, Other than Metropolitan.
	7050 State Planning.
	7070 National Planning.
	7090 World Planning.
7140	Environment. Ecosystem. Analysis. Studies.
7400	Agriculture, Farming.
7950	Water Resources and Conservation.
8040	Power and Energy.
8100	Industry, Trade, Services, Management.
8250	Correctional, Police.
8300	Transportation and Communication.
8600	Demography.

the results of this classification is to negate the necessity for form letters and form subdivisions, such as those found in the Glidden and Marchus classification. A second result is that call numbers are highly specific to the document they identify, which is not necessarily the case with the Glidden and Marchus scheme or the DDC. In some instances in the Harvard scheme, class numbers have been subdivided using decimals, but there are never more than two digits beyond the decimal point. Again, these are peculiarities similar to the LC Classification. In fact, since the Harvard Scheme and the LC Classification have so many similarities in principle and application, most of what was said in the earlier discussion of the LC Classification also applies to the Harvard scheme.

The second major division of the Shillaber revision consists of geographical subdivisions taken directly from Table II of the *LC Classification*: *Class N, Fine Arts.*[73] Similar to the geographical arrangements in subclass JS of the LC Classification, the table from Class N allows optional arrangements for United States publications, those arrangements being by region, alphabetically by state, or alphabetically by city. In a major deviation from its parallels to the LC Classification, the Harvard scheme allows documents to be classed in either of two ways. Using the first option, items may be classed by subject, with geographical subdivisions added. In the alternative, documents may be classed first by place, using the geographical subdivisions. Then the subject classes are added to the geographical subdivisions. This feature was present in the 1913 edition, as well as the 1973 revision. It is identical to that unofficial recognition of classification by attraction in the DDC, mentioned earlier in this chapter.

The third section of Shillaber's revision of the Harvard *Library Classification for City and Regional Planning* is the alphabetical subject index. Shillaber gave no indication in the Preface to the classification whether the subject entries in the index are also to be used as card catalog subject headings or whether Library of Congress Subject Headings should be used. In any event, the Harvard scheme's index ranks a poor third, when compared and ranked with the DDC's *Relative Index*, and Glidden and Marchus's "Subject Index." For example, several class numbers are sometimes listed after a subject entry if the subject has several treatments throughout the classification schedules. Just the class numbers are given however, with no indication which treatments are represented by which class numbers. Therefore, the cataloging librarian must examine each class number referenced in the entry to determine which is most appropriate. While the number of these multiple-treatment class numbers averages between two and three per index entry, in some extreme cases it can mean examining five or more class numbers. The index entries under "Environment" and "Recreation" exemplify this situation. Of course, more than half of the index entries list only one class number, but this does nothing to resolve the multiple-entry problem.

The vocabulary used in the index appears to have incorporated some jargon in the field of city planning, as might be expected. Most index entries are either phrases or adjective plus noun forms. The phrase entries most often contain jargon, when jargon is used. The entries that use adjective-plus noun form are distinctly different from their counterparts in the Glidden and Marchus "Subject Index," because the nouns are frequently modified by more than one adjective. The proportion of two-word hyphenated adjectives is also significant. An excellent example, incorporating some of these attributes, is the index entry, "High-cost single detached houses." It combines the uses of jargon, multiple adjectives, and hyphenated adjective. Although there are entries under "Houses, Detached," "Single detached houses," and a "see" reference from "Detached Houses" to "Houses, Detached," the direct entry "High-cost single detached houses" is the only index entry containing the element of "High-cost." It is not given anywhere else. There is no evidence why the entry appears in full form in only one place in the index. If the reason was economy of space, then the usefulness of the original direct entry should have been questioned, since "High-cost" is not a useful entry term.

Many phrases used as entries in the subject index appear to have been manipulated and entered in a manner very similar to the technique used in the articulated indexing method, developed by Michael F. Lynch, of the Postgraduate School of Librarianship, University of Sheffield, England.[74] For example, the entry, "Traffic, Surface, Obstruction by street transit structures, 2357," is an articulated form of the main entry, "Obstruction of surface traffic by transit, 2357." Lynch's articulated indexing works on the principle of writing a phrase in which the key noun entry terms are part of a prepositional phrase. More than one prepositional phrase may be joined together in a "title-like" descriptive phrase. One main entry is then made under the title-like phrase in its exact word order, with subsequent added entries made under the key noun terms. The prepositional phrases are used as modifiers of the key nouns. Thus, in the example used earlier in this paragraph, there was another anticipated entry in the index under "Street transit structures," which in its entirety appeared as, "Street transit structures, Obstruction of surface transit, 2357." If all the subject index entries had been prepared in this fashion, there would have been a solid consistency and predictability among the entries, not to overlook the collocating effects possible with articulated indexing. Instead, the index has inconsistencies such as an entry under "Education, Public," but nothing under "Public Education." There are some so-called "orphans" too, of which "Bridle paths" is a good example. There are neither cross-references to "Bridle paths" nor entries under related terms such as "Equestrian," "Horses," or "Animals." There are entries though under "Trails" and "Riding trails," but only the entry under "Riding trails" gives some hint that there may be a subclass for bridle paths.

There are cross-references in the index, but not in sufficient supply. In short, the index is merely adequate, and appears to have suffered from economies.

It also should be noted that the Harvard classification employs no scope notes. This omission has been considerably mitigated by the enumeration used in development of the scheme's subclasses and should not pose a major problem.

Table 6 sets forth two examples of the scheme's notation, using the same two hypothetical documents employed in the Glidden and Marchus classification evaluation. In the example of the church construction document, NAC 3590 is representative of the class, "Religious Buildings," while .287 is the geographical table's representation of Santa Monica, assuming the documents are arranged alphabetically by city. The notation for the Los Angeles County budget document is composed of the class number NAC 7010.3, representing "County Planning Administration," plus 28, the latter being the geographical representation for Los Angeles when documents are arranged alphabetically by county name. The development of the geographical portion of the notation involved some interpolation of digits, just as if the LC Classification tables were being used. The year has been added to the budget document to bring about a chronological shelving sequence.

Table 6.
A Library Classification for City and Regional Planning, Harvard University, Graduate School of Design—Examples of Notation

Document Description	Notation
Report on the Construction of the Buildings to House the Church of Sacred Knowledge Center, in Santa Monica, California	NAC 3590.287
Annual Budget of the Planning Board of Los Angeles County, California	NAC 7010.328 1982

Shillaber has mentioned that the use of the mnemonic "NAC" is optional.[75] Those libraries already using the LC Classification may wish to use "NAC" to indicate the subgroup of documents classed under the Harvard scheme. In a library using the LC Classification, these documents, if integrated with the general collection, would be shelved following LC Class "NA," Architecture. It is important to note that the Harvard classification, when used in an integrated setting, would achieve maximum benefit when used in conjunction with the LC Classification.

With reference to the County Planning Budget in Table 6, it should be noted that county documents have been allocated classes 7000-7029. In any shelf arrangement then, *all* county documents will be shelved together, as would all state, federal, and international documents. In instances where a library collects documents from several levels of local government, the grouping by type of government in the Harvard scheme would not provide as complete an array of documents on a specific subject as would be provided by the DDC or Glidden and Marchus schemes. The DDC and Glidden and Marchus schemes first class all documents by subject, then subdivide by level of government. By arranging documents first by level of government, the Harvard classification has adopted one of the attributes frequently seen in archival document arrangements. It may be said, therefore, that the Harvard scheme will group some documents by level of government and scatter subjects through each of those levels. On the other hand, the DDC and Glidden and Marchus schemes will gather all documents from every level of government and group them by subject, but in doing so, will scatter documents from any given level of government. This condition will have greatest effect on large, diverse document collections, rather than on small and homogenous ones.

As can be seen from Table 6, the call numbers for documents, if used without the mnemonic, would be considerably shorter in length when compared with their counterparts in the DDC or Glidden and Marchus schemes. The call numbers are highly similar to, but slightly shorter than, a comparable LC class number, because LC lengthens its numbers by adding book numbers to the class marks. The shorter numbers of the Harvard scheme might speed shelving operations and create less confusion among users when searching for a document.

The Harvard classification has anticipated possible expansion ever since the first edition in 1913. As a result, whole blocks of class numbers still remain unused, and users of the scheme would have to pencil in new subject areas, which was the practice followed at Harvard between the 1913 and 1973 editions. The length of time between revisions of this classification is another measure to weigh when selecting a classification scheme. Librarians who prefer to have more frequent revisions would most likely be more satisfied using the DDC or LC Classification.

When contacted recently, Christopher Hail, the Assistant Librarian at the Frances Loeb Library at Harvard's Graduate School of Design replied that the library no longer uses Shillaber's classification and has no plans to revise it. The library has used LC Classification since 1978. Therefore any library considering the adoption of this classification would have to use it as it stood in 1973. Revision and updating would become an in-house operation. It is probably fair to say that the amount of work needed to maintain the Harvard classification would be in proportion to the size of the library's documents collection. Libraries considering adoption of the Harvard scheme should assess their own collections of local documents, and determine how well the Harvard scheme accommodates the collections.

Incorporated into the assessment should be a projection of the collection's anticipated growth. The results should give a fair idea whether the Harvard classification is the road to follow.

Vivian S. Sessions, "The City Planning and Housing Library: An Experiment in Organization of Materials," *Municipal Reference Library Notes* 37 (November 1963): 269-283.

The classification developed at the New York City Planning and Housing Library is suitable for a separate collection of local government documents. The scheme was designed largely for a collection of planning documents, but, like the Harvard classification, is capable of accommodating a larger spectrum of selected documents from the local, state, county, and regional levels of government.

The classification was developed in 1961 by Thelma Smith, then Deputy Municipal Reference Librarian at the New York City Municipal Reference Library. Refinements in the classification were still being made when part of it was published in 1963. Throughout its development and first two years of use, Smith consulted with attorneys, architects, economists, sociologists, professional planners, and subject experts.[76]

To the extent these professionals were consulted, the scheme reflects their preferences and requirements, as well as reflecting the composition of the library's collection, the latter having begun with some materials provided by the New York City Municipal Reference Library and the City Planning Department. This core collection was developed to serve the needs of the City Planning Commission, the Housing and Redevelopment Board, and the Departments of Real Estate and Relocation.

The outline of the New York City Planning and Housing Library (NYCP&HL) Classification makes it quite evident that department professionals' needs shaped it. The scheme's class schedules lack the scope and depth of Shillaber's Harvard scheme, the Glidden and Marchus classification, and, of course, the *Library of Congress Classification* Class N. While the subject areas covered are similar, the tailoring of the NYCP&HL Classification to the wishes of its users and the constraints of its collection make direct comparisons strained. For example, subjects such as Land Use and Community Facilities form whole classes in the NYCP&HL Classification, while they are treated as less important subclasses of broader subjects in the LC, Harvard, and Glidden and Marchus classifications. Another subject area, Educational Facilities, is treated as a subclass by the NYCP&HL Classification, while it comprises a whole class in the Harvard scheme. This is not to infer that the NYCP&HL Classification is inadequate for all collections, but rather to point out that it has a certain in-house emphasis that the other three subject schemes do not approach.

As a result, librarians considering use of the NYCP&HL Classification to arrange a municipal documents collection should compare the composition of their collections with the scheme's major classes. The amount of material in any given collection that falls outside these classes will give a fair idea of how much work will be needed to develop the classification's unused classes to meet the needs of the local collection. When Smith developed the scheme, she left sufficient areas for expansion, so that a library with a more diverse collection would have room to maneuver with the class schedules. The twelve main classes are set forth in Table 7.

Table 7.
New York City Planning and Housing Library Classification—Main Classes

A	General Reference
B	Planning
C	Area Planning
D	Land Use and Controls
H	Housing: General Data and Special Problems
J	Housing and Urban Renewal: Role of Government
L	Land Economics: Housing and Renewal Finances
M	Social and Economic Planning Factors
N	Neighborhood Studies (NYC materials only)
P	Public Administration and Finance
R	Community Facilities, Utilities and Services
T	Transportation

Source: "The City Planning and Housing Library: An Experiment in Organization of Materials," Vivian S. Sessions, *Municipal Reference Library Notes*, Vol. 37, November 1963, p. 271. Used with the permission of The New York Public Library.

After a class letter has been assigned to a document, Arabic numerals are added to indicate subclasses. A few subclasses have been further subdivided, by using decimal subdivisions, similar to those used in the LC, Harvard, and Glidden and Marchus classifications.

Next, a standard form number is added. The standard form subdivisions are patterned after those used in the DDC, and are divided into four tables, which are applied in accordance with the nature of the document in hand. For example, documents of a general nature would use form subdivisions from Table I, while documents dealing with legislation would receive a form number from Table II. The four form subdivision tables are displayed in Table 8.

Although Smith did not mention using a Cutter number for each document's title, it would be wise to add one, and thereby avoid having the same call number on separate documents dealing with the same topic. Even then, there is a possibility that some documents may have identical call numbers, if their subject, form, and titles are similar. Adding the Cutter

Table 8.
New York City Planning and Housing Library Classification—Tables of Standard Form Subdivisions

Table I

General Subdivisions:
.1   Bibliographies
.2   Research
.3   Conference and seminar papers
.4   History
.5   Executive documents ⎫   For those materials not better classified
.6   Hearings   ⎬   under legislative histories
.7   Legislative documents ⎭

Table II

Legislation Subdivisions:
.1   Laws, statutes, etc., text and summaries, by year
.2   Pending legislation
.3   Legislative histories, by year
.4   Case law

Table III

Agencies Subdivisions:
.1   Periodical reports
.2   Structure
.3   Internal administration
.4   Rules and regulations
.5   Contracts
.6   Minutes
.61 Calendars
.7   Newsletters
.71 News releases

Table IV

Citizen Participation Subdivisions:
.1   Periodical reports
.2   Newsletters, news releases
.3   Conference programs and proceedings
.4   Citizen action guides

Source: "The City Planning and Housing Library: An Experiment in Organization of Materials," Vivian S. Sessions, *Municipal Reference Library Notes,*, Vol. 37, November 1963, p. 283. Used with the permission of The New York Public Library.

number reduces the possibility, but does not eliminate such occurrences. The type of notational specificity found in the LC Classification and Harvard scheme cannot be matched by the NYCP&HL Classification.

Based on her consultations with urban planners and other professionals, Smith found that their preferences were to have documents arranged first by issuing city, county, or region, then subarranged by subject. So instead of adding a geographical subdivision at the end of the notation, Smith placed the geographical name of the issuing city, county, or region in front of the call number. This feature allows for one continuous alphabetical arrangement by the names of the issuing political units. The only other scheme examined in this book which produces an identical straight alphabetical arrangement is Mina Pease's *Plain "J"* Classification. Thomas Heenan's University of Nebraska Classification does produce a continuous alphabetical arrangement for local government documents, but falls short of a complete comparison because the Nebraska scheme does not provide for county or regional documents. The State University of New York at Albany Classification uses a similar approach of geographical subdivisions followed by subject subclasses. However, the Albany scheme ties subject areas to specific agencies and agency subunits, which the NYCP&HL Classification does not. Since it makes an agency-subject association, the Albany scheme has been reviewed in this book as an archival classification because archival schemes place more emphasis on the issuing agencies in their arrangements than do the subject classification schemes.

The NYCP&HL Classification's practice of placing the geographical subdivision at the beginning of the call number is opposite in practice to the other subject schemes, namely the DDC, Harvard, and Glidden and Marchus classifications, which all place area notations at the end of the call number.

Table 9 illustrates two hypothetical documents classified using the NYCP&HL Classification. The components of the call numbers are indicated beneath the two documents. The scheme provides a notation that is brief, and, in most instances, will supply unique call numbers for every document.

Vivian Sessions, the New York City Planning and Housing Librarian who wrote of Smith's development of the scheme, did not mention whether an auxiliary subject index to the classification had been developed to complement the classification schedules. Sessions wrote of the scheme before it was completed.

Despite the absences of an auxiliary subject index and the necessary cross-references, the classification schedules are still usable. This is because Smith did an excellent job of creating well-organized classes with concise headings that use a controlled vocabulary. The class names are written in classified form, with subclasses appearing as subdivisions of the general class. Thus, subclass names such as Land Use—Mixed, Land Use—Planning, and Land Use—Residential, could easily serve a dual purpose as card catalog

Table 9.
New York City Planning and Housing Library Classification—Examples of Notation

Issuing Agency and Document Title	Notation
Burlington, Iowa. Office of Taxes and Finance. Proposed City Budget for Fiscal Year 1982-1983	Burlington P43.1B85
Fargo, North Dakota. Board of Education. Summer Adult Education Programs, Monthly Newsletter, June 1982	Fargo R27.7S63 6/82

Burlington, Iowa Document: Components
P   Main class: Public Administration & Finance
4   Subclass: Municipal Finance
3   Subclass: Capital Budgets
.1   Form subdivision from Table III: Periodical Reports
B85   Cutter number for Budget as the key title word

Fargo, North Dakota Document: Components
R   Main class: Community Facilities, Utilities and Services
2   Subclass: Educational Facilities
7   Subclass: Adult Education
.7   Form subdivision from Table III: Newsletters
S63   Cutter number for Summer as the key title word
6/82   Month and year of issue

subject headings. Scope notes appear in the form of brief parenthetical explanations after the class name.

Anne M. Gordon, Acting Director of the City of New York Municipal Reference and Research Center, reports that the NYCP&HL Classification was used with only minor modifications through the mid-1970s. The New York City Planning and Housing Library then fell victim to New York City's great financial crises of that era. The library still exists, but in greatly reduced form. The classification scheme is not used, and there are no librarians in charge.

Frederick N. MacMillin, *Library Classification for Special Collection on Municipal Government and Administration* (Madison, Wisconsin: League of Wisconsin Municipalities, 1932).

In 1932, Frederick N. MacMillin, the Executive Secretary of the League of Wisconsin Municipalities, published a classification scheme designed for libraries with extensive collections in the field of municipal government.[77]

MacMillin wrote only a single paragraph introducing the scheme, saying that some portions of it would need further expansion, while others contained detail in advance of needs at that time. No other information was provided as to objectives of the classification, or reasons given why the scheme came into being. Therefore, it can only be assumed that deficiencies in the DDC and LC classifications at that time, in the subject areas of local government and public administration, brought the Wisconsin scheme into being. The DDC and LC Classification schedules' deficiencies had been the reason given for the development of the Jackson Notation and the Glidden and Marchus scheme in the period from 1938 to 1941. The Jackson Notation is discussed later in this chapter.

MacMillin used the basic structure of the DDC as the framework for the League of Wisconsin Municipalities scheme. Main classes and subclasses were based on subdivisions of ten, and employ decimal divisions, as does the DDC. However, there were no subject correlations between DDC classes and classes in MacMillin's Wisconsin scheme. Table 10 sets forth, in abbreviated form, the general outline of classes for the League of Wisconsin Municipalities library classification. As can be seen from Table 10, the scheme begins with general government materials, then moves on to materials relating to municipal officials and administrative offices. Then, beginning with class 300 through class 880, the scheme provides for public planning materials, followed by public services publications. There seems to be a misplacement of classes 300 through 399, Public Safety. These materials precede city planning materials in classes 400-699, and would have a more appropriate position after class 599, closer to other public service classes, such as Public Health and Public Utilities in classes 700-880.

Classes 930-990 also appear to have suffered. They have been treated as miscellaneous and lumped together at the end of the classification. They are underdeveloped, and would require some effort on the part of a library to give some substance to these subject areas. Classes 930 through 960 would have been better placed in other parts of the scheme, and classes 980 and 990, Public Libraries and Schools, should have been expanded into classes of their own. Classes 930 and 950, Courts and Prices Control, would have been better situated under class 110, Municipal Government. Class 940, Crime, should have been a part of class 300, Public Safety.

There are additional difficulties with the scheme. Some of the terminology is dated, particularly in the classes dealing with sanitation and public health. Additionally, MacMillin included no instructions to follow after assigning a class number. There are no lists of form subdivisions (although some classes and subclasses are specific to form and treatment), geographical area notations, codes for different levels of government, or Cutter numbers to be applied. Also missing is an alphabetical subject index to the scheme. Scope notes are parenthetical appendages to class names.

In its favor, the scheme does have a sophisticated system of cross-references. Adequate cross-references, however, do not compensate for the absence of the aforementioned features. This is an incomplete classification that really should not be used for a documents collection unless the library and librarians are willing to take on a lot of work to forge a finished product from what is essentially just a foundation.

A revised edition would be welcomed.

National League of Cities/United States Conference of Mayors, *The NLC/USCM Library Classification System: Index for an Urban Studies Collection* (Washington, D.C.: National League of Cities/United States Conference of Mayors, 1970).

The mastermind behind this classification scheme for federal, state, and local documents was not identified in its Preface. Instead, Raymond G. Roney, Director of the National League of Cities/United States Conference of Mayors (NLC/USCM) Library, bestowed thanks for assistance upon Madeline Baker, Joyce Killian, Kathy Shakotko, Laurence Williams, and Thomas Walker. The scheme was devised by the NLC/USCM Library's "librarian." Whether this meant Roney is not clear. The only objective and explanation of the scheme's inception appeared in two short paragraphs in the Preface. The second paragraph of the Preface reads:

Before any classification system was applied, the subjects were outlined for their own values. No attempt was made to fit the plan to a theoretical notation; the object rather was to make the notation fit the subject matter.[78]

Table 11 provides an abbreviated outline of classes. When it is compared with the League of Wisconsin Municipalities library classification's class outline in Table 10, it shows a definite similarity to the latter scheme, although the organization of classes and names assigned to classes are somewhat different. For example, class 400, Land Use and Development, provides for the same materials in MacMillin's Wisconsin scheme as does the class 400, City Planning, in the NLC/USCM scheme.

The NLC/USCM classification has combined some subjects that were treated separately in the League of Wisconsin Municipalities scheme. For example, classes 600, 700, and 990 of the League of Wisconsin Municipalities classification, namely Sanitation, Public Health, and Schools, appear as one class, 800, Health, Education and Welfare, in the NLC/USCM Library Classification.

Some of the "miscellania" classes at the end of the League of Wisconsin Municipalities library classification also appear in the NLC/USCM scheme, but have been more selectively placed in the latter. For example, the Wisconsin scheme's class 940, Crime, has become part of class 500, Public Safety, in the NLC/USCM scheme. Courts, class 930 in the Wisconsin scheme, has been judiciously assigned to class 100, Government, of the NLC/USCM scheme.

Table 10.
League of Wisconsin Municipalities Library Classification—Abbreviated Outline of Classes

001	Lists of Municipal Officials	500	Public Works
010	Government	510	City Engineering
050	Community Surveys	520	Roads & Streets
100	Municipal Government	530	Traffic Control
120	Municipal Corporations	570	Engineering
130	Municipal Administration	600	Sanitation
150	Regional Government	610	Waterworks
170	Elections	620	Sewage Disposal
180	Public Employment	660	Waste Disposal
200	Finance	690	Cemeteries
210	Budgets	700	Public Health
230	Accounting	730	Pure Food
240	Taxation	750	Communicable Diseases
260	Purchasing	760	Health Control
280	Licenses	770	Child Health
300	Public Safety	780	Hospitals
320	Police Departments	790	Public Welfare
330	Fire Departments	800	Public Utilities
350	Building	810	Electric Utilities
360	Electrical Inspection	820	Gas Utilities
370	Plumbing Inspection	830	Local Transportation
380	Nuisances	840	Railroads
390	Weights & Measures	850	Waterways
400	City Planning	860	Aeronautics
420	City Growth	870	Telephone
430	Regional Planning	880	Radio
440	Zoning	930	Courts
450	Housing	940	Crime
460	City Beautification	950	Prices Control
470	Parks	960	Business Promotion
480	Recreation	980	Public Libraries
490	Horticulture	990	Schools

Other differences exist between the 1932 League of Wisconsin Municipalities library classification and the 1970 *NLC/USCM Library Classification.* The general reference classes, and some subclasses, have been expanded in the *NLC/USCM Library Classification* to reflect the growth in the field of urban studies and changes in municipal government which have taken place in the thirty-eight years between the appearances of the two schemes. For example, NLC/USCM subclasses 810.41 and 810.42,

Water Chlorination and Water Fluoridation, do not appear in the League of Wisconsin Municipalities scheme. The same is true of class 810.5, Air Pollution.

In spite of all these differences, there are still remarkable similarities between the schemes. Table 12 compares classes 330-346 of the Wisconsin scheme with classes 510-510.25 of the NLC/USCM classification as an illustration. In fact, the order of classes and terminology of both schemes

Table 11.
NLC/USCM Library Classification System—Abbreviated Outline of Classes

000	General Reference	700	Public Utilities
	010 Legal Documents		705 Electric Utilities
	020 Directories		710 Gas Utilities
	030 Bibliographies		715 Transportation
	040 Proceedings		720 Telephone Utilities
	050 General Literature		721 Radio
	060 Sociology	800	Health, Education & Welfare
	070 Economics		801 General Works
100	Government		802 Public Health
	110 Federal Government		803 Health Departments
	120 State Government		804 Health Institutions
	130 Local Government		805 Pure Food
	140 Municipal Orgs.		806 Communicable Diseases
	150 Elections		807 Health Control
	160 Municipal Courts		810 Sanitation
200	Finances		811 Cemeteries
	210 State		812 Animals
	220 Municipal		813 Hospitals
	230 Joint Financing		814 Child Health
	240 Licensing		815 Public Welfare
300	Personnel Mgmt./Industrial		820 Education
	Relations	900	Parks and Recreation
	310 Manpower		901 Parks
400	Land Use and Development		905 Recreation
	410 Construction		906 Historic Preservations
500	Public Safety		906.1 Museums
	510 Fire Departments		906.2 Libraries
600	Public Works		
	610 Bridges		

Source: "The NLC/USCM Library Classification System: Index for an Urban Studies Collection," Raymond G. Roney, 1970, National League of Cities, Washington, D.C., pp. 11-23. Used with the permission of the publisher.

Table 12.

Comparison of Classes 330-346 of the League of Wisconsin Municipalities Library Classification with Classes 510-510.25 of the NLC/USCM Library Classification System

330	Fire departments		.4	Flammable liquids
	.1 Rating of facilities		.5	Cleaning and dyeing
331	Reports		C	Laws
332	Manuals		346	Fire—protective equipment
333	Methods of fire fighting		510	Fire departments
334	Fire personnel		.111	Volunteer
	.1 Firemen—training		.12	Department records and reports
	.2 Firemen—examinations			
335	Fire equipment		.13	Fire fighting manuals
336	Fire stations.		.14	Fire fighting methods
338	Salvage work		.15	Personnel
339	Outside fire service		.151	Firemen—training
340	Fire protection		.152	Firemen—selection
	A Bibliography		.16	Equipment
	B Laws		.17	Fire stations
	C Reports		.18	Salvage work
341	Fire prevention		.2	Fire protections
	C Laws		.21	Fire preventions
	.1 Fire prevention—inspection		.211	Inspection—education
	.2 Safety education—fire		.22	Fire insurance
	.3 Fire drills		.221	Fire protection rating
342	Fire insurance		.23	Fire causes
343	Fire—causes		.231	Fire statistics
	.1 Fire—statistics		.232	Arson
	.2 Arson		.233	Liability for fires
	.3 Personal liability		.24	Fire hazards
344	Fire hazards		.241	Explosives
	.1 Spontaneous combustion		.2411	Fire works
	.2 Explosives		.2412	Fire arms
	.22 Fire works		.242	Flammable liquids and gases
	.24 Moving pictures—fire hazard		.243	Cleaning and dyeing
	.3 Dust explosions		.25	Fire protection equipment

Source: "The NLC/USCM Library Classification System: Index for an Urban Studies Collection," Raymond G. Roney, 1970, pp. 14-15. National League of Cities, Washington, D.C. Used with the permission of the publisher.

are so similar that it is difficult at times to see them as two different schemes.

The NLC/USCM classification has an alphabetical index, complete with cross-references, a feature wanting in the Wisconsin scheme. The alphabetical index appears to have been created simply by arranging in alphabetical order all the class and subclass titles. While such an arrangement provides easy entry into the classification schedules through the use of very specific terms, it also can lead to confusion in some instances, since entries that appear to be main classes are sometimes found in the schedules to be a second or third subdivision of an unrelated subject class. A good example of this problem can be seen in two entries in the alphabetical index, Public Buildings—411, and Public Assembly Buildings—511.41. At first glance, Public Assembly Buildings would appear to be a more specific type of Public Building. Upon turning to subclass 511.41 in the classification schedules however, Public Assembly Buildings was found to be a subclass of Public Safety Codes and Regulations—not entirely what was expected. There was no general entry in the index under buildings.

The NLC/USCM scheme has some additional problems. Scope notes in the classification schedules are extremely limited and appear as brief, parenthetical qualifications. Some classes, such as Libraries (906.2) and Education (820), remain underdeveloped, while Sanitation (810) is overcrowded. Also, as with the Wisconsin scheme, the *NLC/USCM Library Classification* provides no standard form numbers, geographical subdivisions, or instructions thereupon. After class numbers are assigned, the rest of the shelf arrangement appears to be left to each library's own discretion.

When the *NLC/USCM Library Classification System* is viewed as a more modern version of the League of Wisconsin Municipalities library classification, it seems to have gone only part way toward correcting some of the deficiencies in the latter. When the NLC/USCM Library Classification is viewed as an alternative to the Wisconsin scheme, it is the better choice between the two. However, the irregularities still inherent in it, combined with incompleteness, place it along with the Wisconsin scheme on the lower end of the scale, if all the other subject classifications thus far examined are included. For a library seeking a subject arrangement for its local government documents, the DDC, LC Classification, Glidden and Marchus, or Harvard schemes provide better choices.

Olivia Kredel, Manager of the Municipal Reference Service at the National League of Cities in Washington, D.C., has informed the author that the *NLC/USCM Library Classification System* is no longer used by her agency. The NLC/USCM scheme has been abandoned in favor of the Glidden and Marchus *Library Classification for Public Administration Materials*. The National League of Cities obtained a copy of the Glidden and Marchus scheme from the U.S. Census Bureau Library. The copy contained all the modifications made to the scheme by the Census Bureau Library over the years. Meanwhile, the National League of Cities continues to make its own updates to the Glidden and Marchus classification outline because a proposed joint revision of it with the Census Bureau never came about. This no doubt had something to do with the adoption of the LC Classification by the Census Bureau Library.

ARCHIVAL ARRANGEMENTS

Raynard Swank, *A Classification for State, County, and Municipal Documents* (Boulder: By the Author, 1941. Mimeographed).

This classification scheme was developed around 1940 at the University of Colorado by Raynard Swank, Documents Librarian. It was designed for use with a separate collection of state, county, and municipal government documents. Swank described its development:

The classification . . . is not new in principle. Like other schemes already in use, it adheres to vertical divisions by issuing office rather than horizontal divisions by subject. It is distinguished mainly by its inclusiveness and its capacity for expansion. Moreover, its basic simplicity allows a person who is familiar with the general arrangement to find specific publications without recourse to an index of call numbers.[79]

An underlying reason for the development of this scheme also rests upon the fact that in the late 1930s, the University of Colorado ceased cataloging its government publications because of financial difficulties. Ironically, the library's document collection was increasing at that time to meet student and faculty research needs. Therefore, while the library could rely on the *Superintendent of Documents Classification* and printed catalogs of federal documents to suffice for its federal government documents, no comparable scheme or indexes were available for the library's forty-two thousand state, county, and municipal documents. Thus, the need developed for a classification scheme whereby documents could be located with a minimum of effort. A shelf list or simple notation were thought the best devices to fill those minimum requirements.[80]

Swank countered objections to the absence of cataloging for municipal and county publications by writing:

Our experience, however, tends to support the theory that most requests for local documents, as well as for state documents, can be defined in terms of the work of some specific agency in a specific locality, in which case the classification alone is adequate.[81]

This statement was accurate at the time it was made in 1941. The growth of government agencies in the United States had begun only a few years earlier as the social aims of President Franklin D. Roosevelt's administration were carried out. World War II saw another expansion of government's role in everyday affairs, and in the forty-two years since Swank's statement, there has been continued growth in government at all levels. Although there may still be some substance left in Swank's statement as far as local government is concerned, it is also obvious that the complexity of local government has increased, along with the volume of publications. The reasons for this trend were discussed in the Preface of this book. Therefore, while it still may be possible to point to a single local agency as the probable source of information to a question posed, if that agency produces a sizable number of publications, it may not be such a simple task to locate the exact publication needed without some form of subject analysis or content indexing of documents.

As pointed out in Chapter 1, Shearer has said that most statistical questions are asked by subject, not by agency name or title of document.[82] The analysis of a library's use of its own collection is important in determining whether an agency arrangement or subject arrangement is to be preferred. The cost-benefits of cataloging documents versus the amount of time spent by reference librarians in locating information should also be a part of such an analysis.

In Swank's Classification, documents are filed alphabetically by state. Each state and territory of the United States has been assigned a number, beginning with the Arabic numeral one. The states of Alaska and Hawaii had not been admitted to the union in 1941; therefore, Swank assigned to them numbers sixty-five and seventy-seven, which places them out of alphabetical order. For a library just adopting the scheme, however, new sequential numbers could be assigned to the fifty states, and libraries that do not collect out-of-state documents need not worry at all about number reassignment at the state level.

In the case of county and municipal publications, the name of the city or county that produced the document is indicated by a Cutter number following the number assigned for each state. County documents are differentiated from municipal documents by placing a capital "C" after the Cutter number indicating the county's name. Swank made no provision for documents of regional commissions, but a capital "R" after the Cutter for city, county, or region name might be used to designate and incorporate these documents into the classification. Such a modification would be in keeping with the scheme's arrangement of documents in large groups according to the level of government at which they are produced.

Once assigned, the state designator number plus the Cutter number for city or county are then followed by a hyphen. After the hyphen, the name of the agency or department that produced the publication is Cuttered, using the first key filing word in the agency's name. This Cutter number may be followed by a capital letter, or letters, to indicate a bureau or subunit within a department or an agency. The letter or letters should be a mnemonic that reflects the first key filing word in the bureau's name. The first line of the classification's notation would be complete at this point.

The second line of a county or city document's notation in the Swank scheme begins with a number which reflects either an issuing office, a particular form of document, or a series number. For example, the numbers 1, A2, A3, A4, A5, and A9 are used to indicate annual reports, council documents, mayoral documents, commission documents, city manager documents, and collected documents respectively. However, any series numbers already provided for the documents by the issuing office or agency may be substituted. The numbers A6, A7, A8, A10, and so forth, provide for expansion and may be assigned as needed.

The series or form number is followed by a colon and then the date. The date is usually indicated by the last three digits of the appropriate year of publication. Use of the date is optional if some other feature is preferred, such as volume and issue, month, quarter, week, or even a Cutter number for the title.

Table 13 uses the two hypothetical documents of previous examples to exemplify the notation for these items developed under the Swank classification. The title of the Santa Monica church document, used in previous examples, has been slightly modified, and assigned to the Planning Department, while the Los Angeles County Budget has been described as a budget for the entire county, rather than for the Planning Department alone. The components of the document call numbers from Table 13 are set forth in Table 14.

As can be seen in Tables 13 and 14, Swank's Classification is simple in application. It is possible that assignment of call numbers could be turned over to a clerical staff member. The filing sequence of document call numbers is easily mastered also. For each state, state documents are filed first, followed by municipal documents, then county documents. Municipal documents are subarranged, with council and executive documents filed first, followed by agency documents in alphabetical order by name of agency. This type of alphabetical arrangement does not attempt to reflect the structure of the government, or relationships between agencies, other than placing bureaus and other unit subdivisions to the right of the agency or department to which they are subordinate. This has the effect of reducing the amount of reclassification necessary when subunits of government are shifted in the bureaucratic hierarchy. In fact, in some cases, Swank's scheme may eliminate the need for reclassification, especially if an agency is shifted from one department to another without any name change. Hence, through such observations, it becomes evident that Swank's Classification is more a convenient shelving device than it is an array of documents according to some overall taxonomic design. Of course, its convenient shelving properties met the needs of the University of Colorado in 1941.

The call numbers in Table 13 are brief in comparison to the seven subject classification schemes heretofore reviewed. Yet, of the two documents in

Table 13, only the county budget has a call number that is highly specific. The Santa Monica church building environmental impact report is specific only to the agency and type of document, which seems in keeping with the function Swank intended the classification to perform. Use of a Cutter number for the title of the church document, instead of designation by year, would make for a more specific call number if desired.

Table 13.
A Classification for State, County, and Municipal Documents, Raynard Swank—Examples of Notation

Document Title and Issuer	Notation
Environmental Impact Report on the Construction of the Buildings to House the Church of Sacred Knowledge in Santa Monica, California.	4S59-P692 A6:982
Planning Department of the City of Santa Monica, 1982.	
Annual Budget of Los Angeles County, California. County Auditor, 1982	4L78C-Au2 1:982

Table 14.
Explanation of Notation for Documents in Table 13

Santa Monica church document

4	indicates number assigned to State of California
S59	Cutter number for Santa Monica
-	hyphen
P692	Cutter number for Planning Department
A6	Form number assigned to Environmental Impact Reports
:	colon
982	Year

Los Angeles County Budget

4	indicates number assigned to State of California
L78	Cutter number for Los Angeles
C	used to indicate a county document
-	hyphen
Au2	Cutter number for Auditor
1	Form number assigned to Annual Reports
:	colon
982	Year

The degree to which call numbers should be specific has been a topic of discussion among classificationists for some time. When presented in terms of an arrangement by issuing agency, the arguments sometimes favor less specificity. Everett J. Johnson of the Library of Congress has reported a suggestion by Philip Van de Voorde of Iowa State University that classifications such as the *Superintendent of Documents Classification* should become less specific so as to become more stable.[83] The stability to which Van de Voorde has referred implies no grouping of documents beyond the second governmental subdivision, the idea being that governmental reorganization at the third level subdivision and beyond would not require reclassification of documents. Reorganization of governmental departments, and the havoc it plays with library document collections, has been a source of some concern for government documents librarians because most libraries organize their documents collections by issuing agency and not by subject.

Of course, Van de Voorde has suggested some other order below the second subdivision, such as arrangement by type of document (as was seen in the Swank Classification), or shelved alphabetically by title (a procedure of some schemes to be discussed later in this chapter). The logical rebuttal at this point is to abandon use of the classification if it is not going to be used to bring about some formal order or purposeful relationships between documents. An arrangement by accession number would serve almost as well as a less specific arrangement by issuing agency. The less specificity and predictability an agency arrangement displays, the more it will become dependent upon detailed cataloging and subject analysis to locate documents in the collection. Ironically, cataloging and subject analysis are two of the library tasks that traditionally are supposed to be reduced or eliminated by agency classifications.

Of course, there are arguments in favor of classifying by the archival principle of provenance. Southern Illinois University faculty member, Doris Cruger Dale has described some of the advantages, such as simpler notations and economy of processing.[84]

The main disadvantage of an archival shelf arrangement is separation of material by subject if different departments publish documents on the same topic. Even schemes with subject arrangements find subject scatter inescapable, however, usually because of built-in biases toward treatment of material, such as seen in the LC Classification's use of literary warrant, or because the classification hierarchy is insufficiently detailed, as sometimes is the case with the DDC. Therefore, to fault schemes such as the *Superintendent of Documents Classification* or Swank's Classification on the problem of subject scatter is not as serious an indictment as it would be if made against schemes such as the Harvard or Glidden and Marchus classifications.

Returning to the problem of restructuring government agencies, Everett

J. Johnson has summarized the statement Helen Schroyer of Purdue made in regard to the several policies a library could adopt toward reclassification:

The library may respond either by continuing to file new publications into the old arrangement, change the old publications to the new class number for the issuing office, or leave the old where they are and file the new under their own number and use cross references to get from one to the other. Each of these choices involves varying degrees of labor, expense, confusion, or violation of the archival principle.[85]

Since the sizes of local documents collections were found to be 500 or fewer documents in 80 percent of the libraries responding to both the Nakata and Robinson surveys, the effects of changes in governmental structure would not appear to be devastating for a small separate collection of local documents arranged by provenance.[86] Therefore, the fear of a major reclassification need not become a cause for reduced specificity either in the classification or the notation, unless the collection is unusually large.

There are no recent surveys which would indicate how many libraries might be using the Swank Classification. However, a published article concerning classification of government documents, written by Linda Siler-Regan, Charles McClure, and Nancy Etheredge did refer to a 1958 survey which found the Swank Classification was being used in two state libraries and was about to be implemented in two more in a field of thirty-one respondents.[87] Mr. Swank, now retired from the Graduate School of Library and Information Science at University of California, Berkeley, has told me he knew of six to eight university libraries that were using the scheme for their documents collections.

Ellen Pauline Jackson, "A Notation for a Public Documents Classification," Library Bulletin no. 8 (Stillwater: Oklahoma Agricultural and Mechanical College, 1946).

Ellen Jackson's Notation was designed for international, territorial, foreign, federal, state, interstate, county, and municipal documents. This notation was begun by Raynard Swank in the late 1930s, before he left Oklahoma Agricultural and Mechanical College to become Documents Librarian at the University of Colorado. Jackson, who finished the remaining work on the notation, emphasized that it was merely a so-called "mark it and park it" device to show location of any governmental unit's publications in relation to the other units of a collection of public documents.[88] In spite of her admission in favor of showing relative shelf location of documents rather than vertical hierarchical divisions, Jackson did tamper with the notation to reflect the hierarchies of agency subunits, such as her example of assigning number 186 to the Bureau of Accounts, so that its publications would file immediately after its overseeing agency, the

Fiscal Service, number 185. Jackson's idea in such cases was flexibility to manipulate the notation " . . . to place material in any desired relative location."[89]

The notation consists of several lines of mnemonic letters and numbers. The first line of the notation indicates the class number and first hierarchical subdivision within the governmental bureaucratic structure. Each successive line of notation represents an additional subdivision of governmental authority, except for the last line, which is a book number, the title of which is Cuttered.

In Class M of Jackson's Notation, which contains state, county, and local documents, all states and territories of the United States are arranged alphabetically, and then assigned up to four different numbers for each state. Numbers with terminal zeros are omitted. For example, the state of California might be assigned the following numbers: M18, M19, M21, and M22. Each of the four assigned numbers holds a different class of documents. Class M18, for example, would hold all colonial or republic documents produced prior to California's admission to the United States; M19 would hold all California state documents; M21 would contain all California county documents, and M22, all California local documents.

Table 15 gives examples of seven hypothetical California county and local government documents, along with their respective notations as derived from Jackson's Notation. The titles of the documents in Table 15 are displayed to reflect the governmental hierarchy of the issuing agency or subunit. The first line of each document's notation consists of the main class number, plus the first hierarchical subdivision. The main class marks are either M21 for county documents or M22 for municipal documents. Following the class numbers, the first subdivisions are two-letter mnemonics for the names of the cities or counties in which the documents originated. Jackson has allowed for a certain amount of modification to these mnemonics. Ideally, the mnemonic should consist only of one letter, that being the second letter of the first key filing word in the name of the city or county. This rule is apt to cause some problem, however, in certain instances. For example, with so many proper place names in California beginning with the words Los and San, libraries collecting documents from a number of California cities might have a filing problem, since the first subdivision mnemonic would be O or A in too many cases. Large libraries in the Eastern United States and Canada might have the same difficulty if documents were collected from too many localities that had the word New as part of their names. To avoid problems such as these, Jackson allowed three-letter mnemonics or the substitution of a completely arbitrary set of mnemonics. Adjusting of the mnemonics so that documents will be arranged alphabetically by city name is also a provision of the notation. Therefore, in Table 15, the documents of the cities of Loma Linda, Los Altos, and Los Angeles have been assigned the first subdivision mnemonics of LI, LL, and LO respectively, so that they will be shelved in alphabetical order.

Table 15.
"A Notation for a Public Documents Classification," Ellen Jackson—Examples of Notation

Governmental Hierarchy and Document Title	Notation
County of Los Angeles.	M21LO
Planning Board.	P9
Annual Budget.	A71
1982.	1982
County of Los Angeles.	M21LO
Department of Public Social Services.	P17
Education & Training Services Program.	ED4
West Los Angeles Activity Center.	WE5
Preliminary Training Services Report.	P915
1982.	1982
City of Loma Linda.	M22LI
Police Department.	P9
Records Bureau.	RE4
Annual Report.	A71
1982.	1982
City of Los Altos.	M22LL
Police Department.	P9
Detective Bureau.	DE4
Monthly Report.	M76
February 1982.	2-1982
City of Los Angeles.	M22LO
Board of Education.	E9
Black Education Commission.	BL4
Report of Commission on Magnet Schools.	M279
City of Los Angeles.	M22LO
Board of Education.	E9
Foreign Students Service.	FO4
Guide for Korean-Speaking Students.	G94
City of Santa Monica.	M22SM
Planning Department.	P9
Environmental Impact Report on the Construction of the Buildings to House the Church of Sacred Knowledge Center.	C473

The second line of each notational example in Table 15 consists of a letter and number assigned to the agency, department, or bureau one step lower in the hierarchy. The letter used is always the first letter of the key filing word of the unit's name. The words Department, Bureau, Coordinator, Division, and Office are not considered key filing words. The second subdivision notational numbers are assigned in intervals of eight, beginning with the number 9, a practice which eliminates terminal zeros.

In the case of the two County of Los Angeles documents in Table 15, two departments at the second subdivision level began with the letter P. To resolve this situation, the Planning Board document was assigned number 9, and the Department of Public Social Services was assigned number 17. This number assignment distinguishes between departments, as well as keeping the departments in alphabetical order. The large gaps between assigned numbers are representative of a major objective stressed by Jackson, that being the ability for internal expansion within the notation.[90] The possibility of internal expansion is a determinant of a classification's hospitality. The ability to manipulate the alphanumerics of Jackson's Notation has increased its hospitality. This has been enhanced by the ability to manipulate the placement of material, making it significantly easier to make adjustments than in the Swank scheme, as Swank's adherence to Cuttering leaves less room for maneuverability between call numbers.

If a third notational subdivision is needed, it is created by using the first two letters of the key filing word of the governmental unit's name at that level. Arabic numbers are assigned in intervals of four. Using the City of Los Altos document in Table 15 as an example, the Detective Bureau was assigned the notation DE4. Fourth subdivision notations also use the first two letters of the key filing word in the subunit's name. Fourth subdivision numerals, however, are derived by assigning the next higher number beyond the number used in the third subdivision. This has been illustrated in Table 15 by the County of Los Angeles, Department of Public Social Services document. The West Los Angeles Activity Center was assigned the notation WE5, one digit higher than the 4 given to the Education & Training Services Program.

After notations are completed to the necessary number of governmental subdivisions, the documents are Cuttered, using the first key filing word of the title, obtaining the letter and number from the three-figure Cutter-Sanborn table. Following the Cutter numbers, any appropriate month, year, volume, or series number is added. These may be omitted if they are not needed to distinguish a document from other publications.

Although Jackson acknowledged that the notation was lengthy, she recommended that libraries having collections limited to documents of one city or county could shorten the notation by not using the class numbers and first subdivision notational symbols. Libraries with small collections would probably prefer the abbreviated format.

Swank's and Jackson's notations look somewhat similar, even though

Swank relies more heavily on Cuttering. The arrangement of Jackson's Notation, with one line of alphanumeric characters for each governmental subdivision, tends to create a greater variance from Swank's than actually exists. Each scheme's systematic classification of documents in level-by-level subdivisions, along with the separation of county documents, are nearly identical. These patterns, of course, are characteristic of archival classification practices.

The principal difference between Swank's Classification and Jackson's Notation occurs at the last subdivision level, where the Swank scheme arranges documents by form or series, while Jackson's Notation arranges them alphabetically by title. All other subdivisions are basically the same.

The effect of the divergence of the two schemes can best be illustrated by analogy. Using a library's fiction collection as an example, at the last subdivision level, Swank's scheme would separate fiction genres such as mysteries, romances, science fiction, fantasy, and westerns. The books would then be shelved by year of publication—although any arrangement other than this, deemed better suited to the library's needs, would be allowed.

Jackson's Notation, on the other hand, would merge all genres into one group, arranged alphabetically by title. Alphabetical arrangement by title would disperse specific types and series of documents throughout this final subdivisional level, as well as furthering any subject scatter that might already exist. Documents at this final subdivision level of Jackson's Notation might with some certainty suffer from an absence of cohesive arrangement. The primary inference here is that Jackson's arrangement is more dependent upon the use of a card catalog as the hierarchy descends than is Swank's scheme. Arrangement by title does not facilitate access unless the title is already known or can be determined by use of the catalog. Therefore, the use of a card catalog to determine the title would be unavoidable in some cases. Since Swank's Classification was to be used together with a shelf list, without benefit of a card catalog at the University of Colorado, his decision to arrange documents by type at the last subdivison in the hierarchy was necessary to maintain some integrity in the organization of the collection in order to allow easier retrieval. The integrity of the arrangement served the purpose of searching a particular group of documents to locate a specific item if the type of document, but not the title or series number, was known.

Of course, the notion that a classification scheme could obviate the need for a card catalog, or even be a substitute for some elementary form of author and title index, is unreasonable. It would work only in situations where the collection is very small or where any publication off the shelf will suffice. The growth in government and the corresponding increase in government publication have more or less dictated the need for better indexing and cataloging of local government documents.

In summary, the advantages of Jackson's scheme, which rest in its hospitality, its flexibility to indicate relative position of documents, and its detailed notation that is easily applied and understood, far outweigh its major disadvantages of arranging some documents by title and creating lengthy call numbers. It should be able to serve adequately, separate documents collections of all sizes.

> James Rettig, "A Classification Scheme for Local Government Documents Collections," *Government Publications Review 7A* (1980): 33-39.

The University of Dayton, Ohio, has developed a classification solely for all local government documents produced by political units below the level of state government.

In the mid-1970s, the University of Dayton's Roesch Library decided to increase acquisition of local documents. It already had a collection of one thousand local documents and found its in-house classification scheme inadequate for a larger collection.

James Rettig, Assistant Reference Librarian at the Roesch Library at that time, reported that a number of scheme criteria and objectives were established prior to the development of a new classification. The criteria, or guidelines, called for a scheme that would assign a unique call number to each document, allow the creation of a subject index using Library of Congress Subject Headings, and provide for documents published by nongovernmental organizations. The last requirement came about because approximately one-half of the library's local documents collection consisted of documents not published by government agencies. In terms of objectives, the proposed classification had to gather a particular agency's publications under one class number and arrange them alphabetically by title.[91]

The creators of the Dayton scheme examined three existing schemes, namely, the Swank Classification, Jackson's Notation, and the University of Nebraska classification. All three were rejected. Although the Nebraska scheme provided for nongovernmental publications, it was not selected because of its "key city" principle, which was considered to pose potential difficulties when documents were collected from more than one locality. The Nebraska scheme will be discussed in detail immediately following the Dayton Classification.

The Swank scheme and the Jackson Notation were both rejected because neither provided for nongovernmental publications.[92] There is some question concerning how closely the librarians at Dayton examined these two schemes, for both easily could have been modified to accommodate nongovernmental publications. In the Swank classification, publications of nongovernmental agencies could have been indicated by using a capital letter N, similar to the capital letter C the scheme uses to indicate county documents. The name of the issuer would then be Cuttered instead of the issuing government agency's name. Some of the unused form numbers Swank had set aside could have been applied, and in lieu of using the date of publication, the documents could have been Cuttered by title.

Jackson's Notation also could have accommodated all nongovernmental publications in one of the unused main classes which were provided for expansion. In fact, Class O, which Jackson left unassigned, was the same class letter assigned by Dayton to its nongovernmental publications. Additionally, the Jackson Notation brings all of an agency's publications together under one class number, arranges them alphabetically by title, and assigns a unique call number—all of which were features required of the new Dayton Classification.

Although Jackson's Notation was not selected, the University of Dayton set out to create a classification that not only incorporated most of the main features of Jackson's Notation, but ironically has a notation and arrangement strikingly similar to Jackson's. As a result, the University of Dayton's Classification is a reinvention of the wheel, so to speak. The similarities in the notations of both schemes can be judged in Table 16. The Santa Monica Planning Department church construction document, used in previous examples, is shown in Table 16 as its call numbers would appear in both Jackson's Notation and the Dayton Classification.

Table 16.
Example of Similarity of Call Numbers—Jackson Notation and University of Dayton Classification

---

Document Title and Issuer: Environmental Impact Report on the Construction of the Buildings to House the Church of Sacred Knowledge Center. City of Santa Monica, California, Planning Department.

Dayton call number	*Jackson Notation*
MS9	M20SM
PL5	P9
C473	C473

As might be expected, the striking similarities between the two schemes go beyond the mere notational. The Dayton Classification possesses a hospitality for expansion and an ability to express hierarchical relationships equal to Jackson's Notation.

Other features of the Dayton Classification are its class for special district documents, its distinct separation of the class number from the book number (to ease shelving), and its provision for minimal classification, whereby documents may be assigned call numbers only at subordinate levels of the hierarchy.

Table 17 sets forth the main classes and class mnemonics used in the Dayton Classification. Rettig has pointed out that school districts within a single county, municipality, or township, may be placed in Classes C, M, or T, rather than in Class S, which would then be reserved for independent or joint school districts.[93] A library would have to follow Rettig's suggestion if it wanted all publications of one county, city, or town gathered under one class. School district documents then would be dispersed throughout several classes.

Table 17.
"A Classification Scheme for Local Government Documents Collections," James Rettig, University of Dayton—Main Classes

C	Counties
D	Special Districts
M	Municipalities
O	Nongovernmental organizations
S	School Districts
T	Townships

Rettig did not seem to define which special districts would fill Class D. Classing of special municipal tax assessment districts and the like under the appropriate municipality would seem more consistent with the scheme's objectives than using Class D for such publications. Class D then could be reserved for publications of regional agencies such as air quality management districts, transportation services, and the like.

After placing each document in its appropriate class, the Dayton Classification's first subdivision consists of a letter and number to represent each governmental unit. Classes C, M, S, and T always use the first letter of the governmental unit's name, and assign numbers in intervals of eight, beginning with the number 9. If documents from several governmental units having the same initial letter are collected, two letters are assigned in the first subdivision. Assignments of double letters are made so as to keep each unit in alphabetical order. This first subdivision is almost identical in application with Jackson's Notation, except that Jackson always uses two-letter combinations.

In Classes D and O, the first subdivision letter or letters used in the notation are derived from the name of the governmental unit, excluding words from its title which are articles, place names, or geographical terms.

The second subdivision in the Dayton scheme is at the council, department, board, commission, or equivalent level. The notation of this subdivision is derived from the first two letters of the key filing word in the agency's name. Similar to the Swank and Jackson arrangements, articles, and words such as "department" are not used in assigning the notation's letters. Added to these two-letter mnemonics are numbers in multiples of four, beginning with the number 5.

The third subdivision, conforming to the established patterns for archival arrangements, represents the next agency or subunit one level lower in the hierarchy. The notation at this level is solely alphabetical, and consists of two letters from the subunit's name, although arbitrary alphabetical characters may be assigned at this level. The Dayton scheme differs only slightly at this level from the Jackson Notation, in that Jackson's Notation is alphanumeric at this level.

The fourth subdivision of the Dayton scheme in the still descending governmental hierarchy is solely numeric. It assigns numbers in intervals of two, beginning with the number 3. These numbers are assigned so as to keep the agencies at this level in alphabetical order. Again, the Jackson Notation differs by retaining use of combined alphanumeric symbols at this level. The results, however, are not significantly at variance.

Further subdivision can be made, if necessary, using the same alpha-numeric patterns.

After the last line of the notation is assigned, the Dayton scheme requires it to be underscored, so that there is a distinct separation from the book number. The book number is derived by Cuttering the key filing word in the title, using the three-figure Cutter-Sanborn table. Again, this is identical to the manner in which the Jackson Notation derives its book numbers.

Table 18 illustrates the assignment of notational symbols at the respective subdivision levels for the hypothetical Los Angeles County Department of Public Social Services document, previously used in Table 15. Below the breakdown by elements, the call number is displayed in final form, that is, combining the class mark and first subdivision on one line, and the third and fourth subdivisions onto one line.

As can be seen from the foregoing, the Dayton Classification is remarkably similar to the Jackson Notation in its principles of application, arrangement, and notational derivation. The suggestion by Rettig that libraries with small collections of documents from one municipality reduce classification work by eliminating the main class and first and second subdivisions of the Dayton Classification could also be said of Jackson's Notation. The Dayton Classification appears, therefore, to have no superior edge over Jackson's Notation.

The principal disadvantage of the Dayton scheme is that it is limited to publications from forms of local government. While this is of no great consequence to the small library with a small collection of local government documents, in a mid-sized library which has separate collections of federal, state, and local documents, adoption of the Dayton scheme for local

Table 18.
"A Classification Scheme for Local Government Documents Collections," James Rettig, University of Dayton—Example of Notation

Governmental Hierarchy and Document Title	Notation
(Class mark for county documents.)	C
County of Los Angeles.	L9
Department of Public Social Services.	PU5
Education & Training Services Program.	ET
West Los Angeles Activity Center.	3
Preliminary Training Services Report.	P915
1982.	1982
Combined call number.	CL9
	PU5
	ET3
	P915
	1982

documents would require one or two additional schemes to organize state and federal documents. Use of several classification schemes for government documents collections could lead to confusion among library users, misfiling of documents if call numbers were too similar, and an added burden on the reference or documents librarians, who must have a familiarity with two or three classification schemes. Using one scheme, such as Jackson's or Swank's, which arrange both local and state documents, would benefit the library users, catalogers, and librarians. It should be pointed out that any additional benefits from using Jackson's Notation for federal government documents would be questionable, since the use of Superintendent of Documents Classification numbers in the Government Printing Office's *Monthly Catalog of Government Publications* makes arrangements by *Superintendent of Documents Classification* more practical.

In terms of arrangement, there is another element of the Dayton Classification to consider if the library in question collects local documents from other states. They Dayton scheme does not use geographical collocation to the extent it is employed by Swank or Jackson. In its main classes, the Dayton scheme groups documents by form of government, rather than by geopolitical origin. Therefore, since the first subdivison arranges documents alphabetically by name of city, county, or township, publications from Sacramento and San Francisco would be interfiled with those from Savannah and San Antonio if the library collected documents from more than one city. This type of arrangement is identical to arrangements in some classes of the LC Classification which is about as close as an archival and a subject scheme will get. The Swank and Jackson schemes both separate documents of different states before arranging them by level of government. In terms of strict adherence to archival principle, the Dayton Classification would appear slightly askew. The preference for one type of arrangement over another, however, will depend upon the use of the documents by librarians and library users, type of library, size and diversity of the collection, ease of access, amount of cataloging given the documents, and any additional considerations peculiar to the particular library. Perhaps for the smaller local documents collection, where classification and organization are performed by librarians other than the technical services employees, the Dayton Classification would present an excellent, consistent, easy-to-apply archival arrangement, far better than most home-grown classification schemes.

Thomas Heenan, "Classification of Local Publications," *Special Libraries* 65 (February 1974): 73-76.

A classification for a separate collection of local government documents has been devised at the University of Nebraska. It was constructed to accommodate an infinite number of publications, of all types, from communities large and small.[94]

Thomas Heenan, of the Gene Eppley Library at the University of Nebraska at Omaha, has described this classification scheme in terms of its use as an alternative to integration of local documents into the general collection, or their maintenance in a vertical file.

A major focus on this scheme revolves around its "key city" principle, described in Heenan's 1973 journal article. The key city principle involves the selection of one city's governmental structure as a model of organization for all local documents collected by the library. The city selected may be the one in which the library is located or any other arbitrarily chosen municipality. Once chosen, the library must establish in typed or written form an authority schedule of department, agency, and office titles for the key city. The authority schedule is maintained in alphabetical order. Single-letter or two-letter mnemonic codes are assigned to the offices, agencies, and departments of the key city, such as "PD" for Police Department. The mnemonics do not have to be assigned so that the titles are kept in strict alphabetical order. Once a mnemonic is assigned, it is not changed or modified to reflect variation in titles of identical departments in different cities which may have dissimilar names for the same agencies. For example, if the key city's Park and Recreation Department has been assigned the letters "PR," publications from the Playgrounds and Parks Department of another city are still assigned "PR," not "P" or "PP." It was this feature of the key city principle which caused the University of Dayton to reject this scheme from consideration, prior to the development of the University of Dayton Classification.[95]

It is easy to see why Dayton rejected it. Librarians familiar with the key city principle would be aware that all publications from municipalities with parks departments would be listed under the key city's Park and Recreation Department heading, regardless of variant titles. The librarian or library users not familiar with the key city arrangement, however, would be unduly reliant upon the authority schedule to determine which title had been assigned to parks departments. The card catalog would need a number of "see" references from variant titles to the official name of the parks department in the key city. Therefore, the scheme has, in effect, created one corporate author main entry and an equivalent unvarying notational symbol for each type of office, agency, or department from which publications are received. The use of a main entry for authorship, in principle, is far from being indefensible. In this case, however, the degree to which main entries have contorted specificity and decreased "user-friendliness" makes it appear to be one of those so-called arrangements devised by librarians for librarians. Too much emphasis has been placed on consistency of titles and not enough thought given to ease of access, logical application, or systematic arrangement.

Subdivisions of agencies, departments, and offices are indicated by a numeral added to the one- or two-letter mnemonic code. These subdivisions may be added from any city from which documents are acquired, do not have to be arranged in any alphabetical order, and are assigned numerals sequentially as they are added to the authority schedule. Additions to the authority schedule of titles, or title subdivisions, which are not represented in the governmental structure of the key city, are listed with the city of their origin in parenthesis, directly following the title. A portion of a hypothetical authority schedule is illustrated in Table 19, to shed some additional light on the application of these rules.

After the first departmental subdivisions are designated by assigning sequential numbers, any further subdivisions are treated in the same manner, that is, by assigning additional series of sequential numerals for each level of subdivisions. The purpose of the sequential numbering is in keeping with two objectives of the scheme, namely, to provide for an infinite number of documents, as well as being able to accommodate any older documents that might reflect a preexisting organization of the city's governmental structure.

After department mnemonics and department subdivision numeric notational symbols have been assigned to publications, they then are given a designation according to form. The letter abbreviations used to indicate form are listed in Table 20. The listing may be amended as necessary.

After the form of the publication has been designated, either the first word of the title or the key word in the title is Cuttered. Thomas Heenan has suggested Cuttering the key word in the title, since the first word is often a geographical name.[96] This procedure is identical to the University of

Table 19.
University of Nebraska Classification—Hypothetical Authority Schedule

	Authority Schedule
	Key City: New York
BE	Board of Estimate
	Board of Aldermen (Cambridge, Mass.)
	Board of Directors (Phoenix, Ariz.)
BE1	Board of Assistant Estimate
BP	Borough Presidents
BP1	Bronx
BP2	Brooklyn
BP3	Manhattan
BP4	Queens
BP5	Staten Island
CC	City Council
CM	City Manager
CO	Comptroller's Office
CP	City Planning Commission
	Planning Department (Santa Monica, Calif.)
CP1	Redevelopment Authority
CP1/1	Bronx Division
CP1/2	Brooklyn Division
CP1/2/1	Brooklyn Beaches Advisory Committee
CP1/2/2	Brooklyn Heights Preservation Commission
CP1/3	Downtown Redevelopment Committee (Pasadena, Calif.)
LD	Law Department
	Legal Services Department (Philadelphia, Pa.)
LD1	City Attorney's Office (Los Angeles, Calif.)
MT	New York Metropolitan Transit Authority
	Chicago Transit Authority (Chicago, Ill.)
	Southern California Rapid Transit District (Los Angeles County, Calif.)

Dayton Classification's Cuttering of documents in its Special Districts class, Class S. In the case of the Nebraska Classification, it makes sense, since each publication's call number is prefaced with the name of the city or town in which it was produced. Therefore, since the documents would be already arranged alphabetically by city, Cuttering the document by any geographical place name in the title would most likely be redundant.

After the Cuttered key title word, the last three digits of the year of publication are added, along with any other distinguishing volume numbers or abbreviations, such as "supp." for supplement.

Local laws are handled in a slightly different manner. Laws are

Table 20.
University of Nebraska Classification—Letters Used to Designate Publications by Form

A	Addresses, Proclamations, etc.
AR	Annual Reports, Biannual Reports
B	Bulletins, Newsletters, House Organs, etc.
C	Constitutions, Charters, etc.
D	Directories
M	Manuals, Handbooks, etc.
MAP	Maps
MI	Minutes of Meetings
P	Periodicals
PL	Publications Lists
PR	Press Releases
SP	Special Reports

Source: Reprinted from Special Libraries 65 (no.2): 76 (Feb. 1974), p. 76. Used with the permission of the author and Special Libraries Association, New York.

designated by the letter L following the name of the municipality. Each law is then assigned a three-letter mnemonic designation, or in place of the mnemonic, any numbers that already have been assigned to the local laws. Special titles or key words for each law are Cuttered also.

The Nebraska scheme provides for nongovernmental organizations. These documents are handled just like any others, except that a capital letter Z is placed between the name of the municipality and the class mnemonic. This has the effect of collocating all nongovernmental documents at the end of each city or town's shelf grouping of documents. This arrangement differs quite significantly from the Dayton Classification, which places all nongovernmental documents in their own separate class.

Lastly, the composition of the Nebraska scheme's notation differs greatly from those seen earlier in the Swank, Jackson, and Dayton schemes. Rather than a vertical assemblage of row upon row of notational subdivisions, the Nebraska Classification arranges the notation for each document on one horizontal line, with each subdivision separated from the next by a slash, or virgule. As a result, the Nebraska Classification's notation resembles the NYCP&HL Classification's notation more than any other. Table 21 shows the notations of three hypothetical documents in terms of governmental hierarchy and title. The hypothetical authority schedule in Table 19 has been used to assign class letters and subdivision numbers. The hypothetical documents displayed in Table 21 illustrate how confusing the call numbers can appear in final form. Heenan stated that numbers should be filed before letters, but even that rule of thumb can collapse when any more than two or three subdivisions are involved in the filing process. For the small

Table 21.
University of Nebraska Classification—Examples of Notation

Governmental Hierarchy and Document Title	Notation

City of New York.
  City Planning Commission.
    Redevelopment Authority.
      Brooklyn Division.
        Brooklyn Beaches Advisory
        Committee.
          Monthly Newsletter.
            August 1982.
	New York/CP1/2/1/
	B/982/Aug

City of Chicago.
  Chicago Transit Authority.
    Annual Report.
      1982.
	Chicago/MT/AR/982

City of Santa Monica.
  Planning Department.
    Special Report.
      Report on the Construction of the Buildings to
      House the Church of Sacred Knowledge Center.
	Santa Monica/CP/
	SP/C473

collection, limited to documents of one locality, lengthy subdivisions will not, in all probability, arise often enough to create any considerable problems.

Heenan has suggested that an abbreviated notation be used if the number of documents is small for a particular locality. Use of an abbreviated notation, with less specificity, could create the same type of increased dependency on the two tools Heenan has suggested should accompany the collection, namely, a shelf list and a subject index using either key words or regular subject headings. Heenan's suggested use of both a shelf list and key word subject index is generous in terms of the archival classification schemes examined previously, the purposes of those latter schemes having been directed toward minimal use of card catalogs. In the Nebraska Classification, however, the subject index is more aptly termed inevitable than admirable, since the alphanumeric notational designations are sometimes indecipherable without references to the authority schedule or shelf list. That is the major disadvantage of the Nebraska Classification, namely, that the constant use of sequential numerals to indicate subdivisions eventually diminishes the importance of the hierarchical order as call number designations become more vague. In fact, this characteristic of the Nebraska Classification's notation is not unlike the LC Classification's notation, a condition which stems from the sequential assignment of class and subclass numbers, so that the numbers' principal function becomes a means of denoting location only. This can be contrasted with the DDC, where the class numbers not only reflect relative position, but also represent a systematic positioning of items. Of course, the sequential assignment of subdivision numbers achieves the goal of the Nebraska scheme, that is, to handle an infinite number of documents.

A further disadvantage of the University of Nebraska Classification is that it makes no provision for county, regional, or state documents. This shortcoming is not critical to the use of the scheme, but signifies that county, regional, and state documents must be organized in some other manner. It also precludes the use of the scheme to arrange both local and state government documents under one classification system, should a library wish to do so. It is conceivable, however, that certain elements of the University of Nebraska Classification could be adapted for use with county and state documents. For example, a capital letter C could be used to indicate county documents in the same manner a capital letter Z indicates nongovernmental agency documents. For state documents, one state's governmental hierarchy could be used as a "key state." The arrangement it would create would be identical to that created for local government publications.

Mina Pease, "The Plain 'J': A Documents Classification System," *Library Resources and Technical Services* 16 (Summer 1972): 315-325.

The *Plain "J"* Classification is based on a modification of Class J of the *Library of Congress Classification*. It has been developed primarily for large document collections in large libraries, particularly those that use the LC Classification. The *Plain "J"* Classification System provides large libraries with one method of classification for government documents at the international level down to the local government level and thereby eliminates the inconsistencies that arise when a library uses one classification scheme for its United Nations documents, another for federal government documents, a third for state documents, and so forth.

Mina Pease, of the Pennsylvania State University Library, has described this classification's characteristics as employing a numbers system related to the issuing agency, based on archival principle. Other characteristics are the unique call number provided for each document, the distinction given to government document call numbers, and the ability to incorporate any numbering system already in use by government agencies.[97] It should be noted that Pease developed *Plain "J"* as a proposal at Pennsylvania State University Library, but the scheme was not accepted and put into operation by the library's administration.

The classification operates by taking the LC Classification Class J number assigned to a geopolitical body and using that number as the foundation for all publications of that governmental body. These numbers are modified slightly by adding one thousand to any three or four digit number. Also, the S from municipal document subclass JS of the LC Classification is dropped, and a decimal point is placed between the J and the governmental unit number. Therefore LC Classification subclass JS998 for Little Rock, Arkansas, becomes Class J.1998 in the *Plain "J"* Classification. The LC class numbers are assigned on a geographical basis, and, since LC Classification's subclass JS arranges local documents alphabetically by city, that also is the resulting arrangement of the *Plain "J"* Classification.

The base geographical class number is then followed by a decimal point, and what can best be described as an arrangement number. The *Plain "J"* Classification's arrangement numbers, listed in Table 22, were taken in toto from the table for arrangement of documents in LC Classification Class JS13. It can be seen from Table 22 that the arrangement numbers identify documents by form, but not exclusively. For example, while the first three arrangement subdivisions are limited to specific forms of documents, the third subdivision is less specific, and the fourth even more so. They are not similar to the form subdivisions already seen in the Glidden and Marchus, Swank, and Nebraska schemes. This is one of the incongruities that results from creating an archival classification scheme by eclectically extracting elements from a subject classification.

The geopolitical class number and arrangement number complete the first line of the notation and are followed by a colon, which indicates a break in the notation.

The second line of the notation is an item number, not unlike LC Classification's book numbers. There are two options available when assigning the item number portion.

Option one consists of assigning two LC author numbers, one for the name of the governmental subunit, the second for a key filing word in the title of the document.

Option two provides for the use of any official document number already assigned to the publication by the issuing agency. If such a number is used to identify a document, it must be preceded by a capital letter C, which is the same letter the LC Classification uses to distinguish collections of a single series, arranged by serial number, sessions numbers, or dates.

Option two is almost identical to the provision in the Swank Classification's call numbers, except that Swank allowed use of the official number in lieu of standard form numbers, whereas the *Plain "J"* Classification employs both a standard arrangement number, plus any officially assigned number. In spite of the difference, the provision has the same effect in both of the classification schemes, namely, to keep officially designated series of documents together on the shelf.

Table 22.
Plain "J" Classification—List of Document Arrangement Numbers, taken from LC Classification, Class JS13.[98]

United States. Cities, Towns, etc. A-Z
  Under each:
  (1)   Mayor's report (with Department reports)
  (1a)   Inaugural (and other addresses or messages)
  (2)   Council Proceedings
  (3)   Other serials [Collected Documents]
  (4)   Separate documents not elsewhere provided for under subject (by date)

The use of option two could create a situation similar to that seen in the Nebraska Classification, where call numbers consisted of irregular segments of letters and numbers. Use of option one would create a uniform item number on the second line of the notation, but it might scatter series documents by title. So the use of one option or the other becomes a decision between the series documents scatter in option one, versus the collocation of series documents and the advantage of using an official document number, available in option two.

The scheme reserves classes J.3000-J.4000 for interstate agencies and their documents.

County and regional documents are handled in a slightly different manner. The geopolitical class number is assigned exactly as done for cities and towns. Then a Cutter number, representing the name of the county or region, is placed between the class number and arrangement subdivision number. Decimal points on either side of the Cutter number separate it from the class number and arrangement number.

The manner in which the Cutter numbers are used for county and regional documents has an effect on the shelving arrangement of documents encountered previously only in the *New York City Planning & Housing Library Classification.* The general result of both schemes would be that all municipal, county, and regional documents would interfile alphabetically in one array. There would be a difference though. The NYCP&HL Classification would have a continuous alphabetical array of documents of all types. The *Plain "J"* Classification would group county and regional documents at the beginning of each alphabetical letter, followed by city and town documents whose names began with the same alphabetical letter. This is unusual, because all other archival schemes examined up to this point have segregated county and regional documents in separate classes.

Whether this type of document arrangement would benefit the library would depend on the use patterns of documents by staff and library users, as well as whether or not the documents were part of the general circulating collection. From the standpoint of easy browsing, alphabetical arrange-ments would seem to have some benefits to both users and librarians. Li-brarians would probably incur some time savings in instructions for using the documents, since an alphabetical arrangement needs minimal explan-ation. Of course, the library that collects documents from its own locality only would not find much benefit, other than being able to shorten the classification number by eliminating the geopolitical class number.

In assigning the LC author number to indicate the name of the agency that issued the document, option one of the *Plain "J"* scheme is similar to Swank and different from the Jackson, Dayton, and Nebraska schemes in that the LC author number identifies only the uppermost level of the governmental hierarchy. Pease did not state that the first LC author number *had* to be assigned in this fashion, however. Therefore, the agency or subunit used for the purpose of assigning the LC author number is open to interpretation. Pease's examples did not identify any unit lower than the administrative or department levels, however.

While the first LC author number on the second line of the notation identifies the name of the issuing department or administrative unit, a second LC author number reflects a key filing word in the title of the document. To locate a document issued by a bureau or subunit one or two steps down in the governmental hierarchy, the librarian or library user would either have to refer to a chart of the municipality's governmental structure or determine this from an entry in the card catalog. Since Pease had suggested that the classification be supported only by a shelf list and a check-in card file, there would be little choice but to keep a chart of the city government's structure handy, provide better cataloging, or create some auxiliary tool which contained that information.[99] If the first LC author number of the notation were assigned to the subunit lowest down in the hierarchy, then the need to rely on a structural chart would be diminished, as the arrangement of documents would have become more specific. Lack of specificity below the first governmental level may have the advantage of potential immunity to any rearrangement or restructuring of bureaus at lower levels in the hierarchy, and vice versa. It should be obvious by now that arguments for greater or less specific hierarchical notations are applicable to most agency classification schemes.

The *Plain "J"* scheme's practice of assigning a second LC author number to documents, using the key title word, comes closest in application to the Jackson Notation and Dayton Classification, which follow a similar practice with Cutter numbers. The Nebraska Classification, on the other hand, does not Cutter by title if a standard form subdivision serves as an apt description of the document.

Table 23 illustrates several hypothetical documents, with the notations shown twice. The notations in the center column depict the notation in component form, as components relate to portions of the document

Table 23.
Plain"J" Classification—Examples of Notation

Governmental Hierarchy and Document Title	Notation Components	Notation in Final Form
County of Los Angeles.	J.2001.L7.1:	J.2001.L7.1:
Planning Board.	P5	P5B84
Annual *Budget*	B84	
County of Los Angeles.	J.2001.L7.1:	J.2001.L7.1:
Department of Public Social Services.	P8	P8P72
Education and Training Services Program.		
West Los Angeles Activity Center.		
Preliminary Training		
Services Report.	P72	
1982		
City of Santa Monica.	J.2450.5.1:	J.2450.5.1:
Planning Department.	P5	P5C48
Report on the Construction of		
Buildings to House the *Church of*		
Sacred Knowledge Center	C48	
City of Los Angeles.	J.2001.4:	J.2001.4:
Board of Education.	E3	E3K67
Foreign Students Service.		
Guide for *Korean* Speaking		
Students	K67	

description. The far right column shows the notation in final form. The key title words used for the LC author numbers are in italics. The author numbers used are as revised by the Library of Congress in 1972.[100]

In Table 23, although documents of the City of Los Angeles and County of Los Angeles have been assigned the identical geopolitical Class J.2001, the county documents are distinguished by the Cutter number for Los Angeles County, namely .L7. This procedure for county documents was followed as described by Pease. The LC Classification assigns a span of numbers from 1001 through 1010 to the City of Los Angeles, however, and the county documents could just as easily have been assigned an unused city class number such as 2006, that is, 1006 plus 1000. Use of Class J.2006 would have eliminated the need for the Cutter number, .L7, since all City of

Los Angeles documents would have been classed in J.2001, and all Los Angeles County documents in J.2006. This improvisation would have simplified the notation, although it would have changed the shelving order by placing the Los Angeles County documents adjacent to the Los Angeles City documents, rather than at the beginning of the alphabetical letter L. Whether this is for better or worse is an individual library's decision.

In the case of the City of Santa Monica document in Table 23, LC Classification subclass JS had assigned no specific number to Santa Monica. Instead, LC has assigned the number JS1450 to all cities in the alphabetical sequence beginning with San Francisco, and ending with Savannah. Thus, an interpolation was in order, and the number JS1450.5 was assigned to Santa Monica. Adding the required 1000 to the LC class number, the resulting *Plain "J"* class number for Santa Monica became J.2450.5.

The uniform manner in which the *Plain "J"* scheme classes documents only to the administrative or department level is obvious in Table 23. In the second sample document, neither the Education and Training Service Program nor the West Los Angeles Activity Center was represented in the classification's notation. The same held true for the Foreign Students Service in the last document in Table 23. Both are examples of the scheme's decreased specificity when compared to more specific archival schemes, such as Jackson's Notation and the University of Dayton Classification.

The decreased specificity at work in the *Plain "J"* Classification is a feature suggested for use in the *Superintendent of Documents Classification* by Phillip Van de Voorde, mentioned earlier in this chapter. The advantage, of course, is that reclassification is unnecessary for any governmental subunit reorganization occurring below the first level of governmental departments. Yet, the decreased specificity has not destroyed the *Plain "J"* 's goal of providing a unique call number for each document. This latter achievement is in no small part a result of applying a modified LC Classification to gain the benefit of LC Classification's specificity when assigning call numbers. The resulting shelf arrangement, however, is quite unlike that of any archival scheme examined thus far. Depending upon the complexity of the local government's structure, the scheme allows the inter-filing by title of publications from any number of agencies and bureaus below the administrative or department levels. The result is a scattering by title of publications of subunits within any governmental division, while documents similar in form and title, such as budgets, would be gathered together if all used the key word "budget" as the basis for assigning the final LC author number in each document's notation. If such a situation occurred, then all budgets within a major governmental division of a locality would have identical call numbers. This would be more a problem or positive effect, depending on point of view, of libraries in large cities, or libraries with large collections. Nevertheless, it cannot be overlooked.

The *Plain "J"* Classification's roots in the LC Classification have helped equip it with the ability to accommodate large numbers of documents, as well as an ability to be used alongside the LC Classification as a separate collection, or integrated as part of LC Class J. These features, taken together with a reduced need for reclassification in some instances of governmental reorganization, along with its specific call numbers, should make it attractive to large libraries with substantial documents collections.

Its biggest disadvantage is its lack of subject access, something common to most archival schemes. Subject analysis of documents, about which Pease made no mention, would round out the *Plain "J"* Classification to the point where it might have an operative edge over the other archival schemes examined so far. The *Plain "J"* Classification's biggest drawback is that it does not provide for publications of nongovernmental agencies, but possibly could be modified to do so by adding a fifth arrangement number.

J. Gormly Miller, "Classification of Local Municipal Documents," *Library Journal* 64 (December 1939): 938-941.

In the 1930s, J. Gormly Miller, then the Senior Assistant in the Local History Division of the Rochester, New York, Public Library, created an archival classification different from those reviewed thus far. Miller's classification, hereinafter called the Rochester Public Library Classification, is based from the beginning on governmental function, a method Miller believed presented documents from each part of city government in proper perspective with the whole local government operation.[101] After dividing the work of local government into three functions, publications of each office are placed in an arrangement where they are contiguous to those documents of other administrative units performing related functions. The result is a blend of the archival and subject approaches, which lends a shelf arrangement to the scheme best described as quasi-subject. Table 24, which is an abbreviated outline of the classification, gives visual credence to the scheme's patent approach.

Miller's aims in designing this classification were to create an arrangement that was ". . . simple, expansive, and yet adequate to bring together papers commonly consulted together."[102] It resulted in a scheme for a separate collection of county, municipal, and nongovernmental documents, which is logical in its approach, employs a brief but descriptive notation, and provides ample room for expansion. Its logical organization allows its general order to be readily committed to memory, an advantage not easily disputed.

The classification has at least two shortcomings, however. There is an inconsistency in the designation of form subdivisions, and call numbers sometimes fail to achieve maximum specificity. Otherwise, there is an overall simplicity in this scheme that approaches what Svenonius has called ". . . a certain elegance . . ." in some classification schemes.[103]

Table 24.
J. Gormly Miller, Rochester, New York, Public Library Classification—Abbreviated Outline of Classification

CLASSIFICATION SCHEDULE
Governmental Functions

A.   Basic Law
AB.   Local Law
B.   Legislative Branch
        B1.   City Council
               1.   Rules of Order, Manuals, Directories, etc.
               2.   Proceedings of the City Council
D.   Executive Branch

Administrative Functions

E.   Finance. Ordinances
        E2.   Comptroller
               2.   Annual Reports
EB.   Taxation

Service Functions
(Personal Services)

H.   Education
        HA.   Schools
        HB.   Libraries
        HC.   Museums
I.   Safety of Persons and Property.   Ordinances
        IA.   Fire Protection.   Ordinances
        IB.   Police Protection   Ordinances
J.   Welfare.
        JB.   Health.   Ordinances

(General Services)

K.   Works.   Ordinances
        KA.   Planning.   Zoning Ordinances, etc.
        KB.   Engineering & Construction
        KH.   Parks & Playgrounds
L.   Trade, Commerce, and Transportation

Source: Extracts from "Classification of Local Municipal Documents," J. Gormly Miller. Reprinted from *Library Journal*, December 1939. Published by R. R. Bowker Co. (a Xerox company), copyright © 1939 by Xerox Corporation.

A distinct advantage of Miller's Rochester Classification is its immunity to changes in departmental titles and governmental reorganization, that universal concern of all government documents librarians. As long as the newly renamed (or hierarchically reshuffled) department performs the same function, it stays in the same relative position in the scheme. In practice, the new department would be assigned a new class number, in sequential order, so that documents issued under the old name would be filed immediately before those issued under the new name. For example, in the Rochester Public Library's own experience, the City Manager's Office was assigned subclass EA.3. when it took over all the duties of the old Board of Estimate, the latter having been assigned subclass number EA.2.

Another feature of this scheme is the alternative it offers for shelving municipal ordinances. Ordinances may be shelved in their entirety in subclass AB.2. Alternately, portions of the ordinances may be shelved at the beginning of each class to which they relate.

Unfortunately, Miller did not apply a uniform system of numbering to the many subdivisions in the scheme. The subdivisions, which also are not free floating, vary from class to class. As a result, form subdivision ".1" may indicate "annual reports" in subclass D1, while it is meant to indicate "Rules and Regulations" in subclass G1. Although such a lack of consistency is not critical to the classification's application, it does inhibit performance, since the inconsistencies complicate cataloging, destroy systematic arrangement by form of document within classes, and prevent librarians from using subdivision numbers as memory aids.

Another potential difficulty with the scheme is its chronological arrangement of documents at the bottom subdivision level of the classification hierarchy. The scheme makes no provision for alphabetical arrangement by title, or key title word, as do some of the other archival schemes. Therefore, in the Rochester Classification, often the next step downward from the form subdivision is the date of publication. This has the effect, in some instances, of assigning identical call numbers to different publications. For example, all periodicals published by the local Bureau of Health in 1982 would be assigned the call number JB2.4.1982. The only other scheme examined so far that made so large a hierarchical leap in the classification procedure was the Swank Classification. Swank arranged documents by date after assigning a form number, series number, or Cutter number for title. While the chronological feature in Miller's scheme makes for a slightly easier reshelving of documents than using some other form of organization, such as alphabetical arrangement by title or personal author, it nevertheless presents a problem with retrieval, particularly if an agency produces a sizable number of documents each year that receive the same call number. Furthermore, Miller stated no provisions for undated documents. It would be wise, therefore, to modify this classification slightly and create a subarrangement by title, key word, or personal author before assigning the date of publication.

A question might also be posed about the value of a functional division of local government agencies, as opposed to an alphabetical arrangement of agencies. The Swank, Jackson, Dayton, and Nebraska schemes all employ an alphabetical arrangement of agencies. The *Plain "J"* scheme also had, in essence, an alphabetical arrangement, although it did employ a document arrangement number. The *Plain "J"* arrangement number was related to the nature of the document, however, rather than to the function of the issuing agency, the latter being the case with the Rochester Public Library Classification. From a browsing viewpoint, in a collection having public access, the functional arrangement of the Rochester Classification makes sense, since it displays documents in relative positions, similar, but not identical, to what the DDC does. Arrangement by function also implies that the librarians have given some thought to the organization of the documents. If the collection of local documents is closed to the public, however, the functional arrangement has no particular advantage over the alphabetical arrangement because there will be little or no browsing.

In its notational structure, the Rochester Public Library Classification first uses a single alphabet letter to represent a function of government. Subdivisions of those functions, which are usually departments, agencies, or offices, are indicated by adding another letter to the function letter. These second alphabet letters are not assigned with any intent to keep departments in any particular order.

Descending in the governmental hierarchy, the next level of governmental subunits is represented by a single Arabic numeral, assigned in sequential order. A decimal point follows this subdivision. Documents are then arranged by form, the documents' forms also being indicated by Arabic numerals.

Further subdivisions, usually indicating a specific treatment, such as a history, are sometimes added. If used, such subdivisions are designated by lowercase alphabetical letters.

The last element of the notation, always required, is the date of publication. All these classification subdivisions, except publication dates, are exemplified in Table 25, which presents subclass HA in full.

Neither the Rochester Classification notation nor the class hierarchies provide for inclusion of documents from other communities. Therefore, libraries that collect documents beyond those of their own locality would have to incorporate some form of adaptation in the way of a symbol or an added class. A simple solution might be to assign each community a locality number, which would be used as a prefix to the class number of each document.

Collecting documents from other localities might require a supplementary classification schedule, particularly if the forms of government differed significantly. If this were the case, the library in question might be wise to choose another scheme.

Table 26 illustrates the classification of two hypothetical local documents, using Miller's Rochester Public Library Classification. The middle column in Table 26 lists the notation in component form, while the far right column shows the notation in final form. In the City of Santa Monica document in Table 26, subclass KA2. represents Division of Planning documents as part of broader Class K, Planning. Special reports

Table 25.
J. Gormly Miller, Rochester, New York, Public Library Classification—Subclass HA

HA.   Schools.
HA1.   Special commissions, etc.
HA2.   Board of Education.
    .1 Rules and regulations, by-laws, etc.
    .2 Manuals, directories, catalogs.
    .3 Annual reports.
    .4 Proceedings.
    .5 Periodicals.
    .6 Textbooks.
    .7 Reports, studies, surveys, etc., of the school system, or parts of it, e.g.,
       High schools, Junior high schools, Elementary schools.
    .8 Special publications.
       a. History of the public schools.
       b. Finance. Budgets, etc.
       c. Buildings.
       d. Curricula. Courses of study, etc.
       e. Teaching staff.
       f. School libraries.
       g. Student body. School census, attendence, etc.
       h. Special activities.

---

in sublass KA2. are represented by subdivision .3. Readers will be able to decipher the composition of the City of Los Angeles document's notation by referring to the Class HA outline in Table 25.

It is evident in both examples in Table 26 that the Rochester, New York, Public Library Classification results in a brief notation, possibly the briefest seen thus far. Only Shillaber's Harvard scheme, among those examined thus far, has produced so compact a document description. This is no accident. The detail in both the Harvard and Rochester classification schedules eliminates constant need for adding standard subdivisions to indicate form, geographic location, and treatment. Both schemes achieve their goals with a maximum of simplicity and a minimum of confusion.

H. Holdsworth, "An Arrangement for Government Publications,"
East African Library Association Bulletin 1 (January 1962): 15-25.

The Makerere University College Library, in Kampala, Uganda, has devised a classification scheme for libraries that collect a large number of government documents, from the international level of government down to the municipal level. H. Holdsworth, of the College Library at Makerere University, has written that the college sought a classification scheme that

Table 26.
J. Gormly Miller, Rochester, New York, Public Library Classification—Examples of Notation

Governmental Hierarchy and Document Title	Notation Components	Notation in Final Form
City of Los Angeles:		HA2.4.1982
Board of Education.	HA2.	
Proceedings.	.4	
1982	.1982	
City of Santa Monica.		KA2.3.1982
Planning Department.	KA2.	
Special Report on the Proposed		
New City Hall.	.3	
1982	.1982	

would allow documents to be registered and classified quickly, then cataloged at a later date.[104]

Holdsworth reported that the university's faculty, upon consultation, indicated a preference for a separate collection of documents, with an arrangement by country or issuing organization. Holdsworth said nothing about student preferences, or whether they were sought.

The result was that documents of international organizations were arranged either by the name of the organization or by the name of the country of origin, if the latter were practical. This duality of arrangement with international documents is applied less frequently among national, state, provincial, and local government documents. At the municipal level, documents have been organized to reflect not only the name of the municipality, but also the names of the nation, province, state, or region.

The classification of local documents under the University of Makerere scheme is relatively simple. Each document is prefaced with a capital letter G to indicate that it is a government publication. Then, a two- or three-letter mnemonic code is assigned to indicate the country of origin. The capital letter Z is added to the mnemonic to distinguish municipal (local) publications. It would appear that any library using the classification could group publications from county and regional agencies under the same letter Z used for municipal publications. There would be nothing, however, to stop a library from using different letter designations for county and regional publications, in order to group them into classes of their own, if so desired. The latter choice is preferred by the University of Makerere Library.

Next, the classification applies LC Classification author numbers. Two author numbers are assigned, the first to the name of the issuing city or town, the second to the name of the department, agency, or office from which the document was issued. Further governmental subdivisions can be indicated by adding additional single digits to the appropriate LC author number. All this is followed by a standard form number, enclosed in parentheses. Table 27 is a list of the standard form number subdivisons used by the scheme. Official publication numbers assigned by the issuing agency may be substituted in place of the standard form subdivisions, if their substitution would lend more integrity to the arrangement of the collection. Following the standard form subdivisions, documents may be assigned a sequential accession number. A master catalog is maintained, which contains all assigned call numbers.

Table 28 illustrates two hypothetical documents classified by the Makerere University College Library Classification. The center column in Table 28 lists the notation as the components relate to the document and issuing agency.

Table 27.
Makerere University College Library Classification—Document Form Subdivisions

02	Monographs
05	Periodicals
058	Annuals
08	Collections

Table 28.
Makerere University College Library Classification—Examples of Notation

Issuing City and Agency, and Document Description	Notation Components	Notation in Final Form
City of Milwaukee,		GUSZ.M5T7(08)9
Wisconsin.	M5	
Municipal Transit District.	T7	
Traffic Patterns in Suburban Milwaukee.	(08)	
Accession number.	9	
City of Racine, Wisconsin.	R3	G USZ .R3L5(02)5
Public Library.	L5	
History of the Racine Public Library.	(02)	
Accession number.	5	

Although Holdsworth made no mention of using an abbreviated form of the classification, it can be seen from Table 28 that the full call number might not be necessary for a library with a collection of documents limited to its own community. For libraries with limited collections, use of the letters "USZ" to indicate a city in the United States might be eliminated. Indeed, even the first LC author number, representative of the city's name, might be omitted, leaving a very brief, but nevertheless unique, call number. The individuality of the call numbers is assured by the issuance of sequentially assigned accession numbers to the publications of each department.

According to Holdsworth, the Makerere University College Library maintains two card files for its documents. One card file, which is called the Registration File, is created during the processing of the documents. This card file is kept in shelf number order, so that it is possible to determine which numbers have been assigned. A shelf list of this type is common to most classification schemes. The shelf list, or Registration File, should also indicate if the publication has been shelved somewhere in the library outside of the documents collection.

The second card catalog created by the Makerere University College Library is a public catalog, adjacent to but separate from the main card catalog. This catalog is a general listing of corporate authors and holdings in the documents collection. For example, an entry in the public catalog might contain a card reading, "Milwaukee, Wisconsin—Municipal Transit District—Collected Documents." The library user would have to request a librarian to look at the Registration File to determine if the specific publication exemplified in Table 28 was among the documents collected from the Milwaukee Municipal Transit District, and therefore in the library's documents collection. This type of cataloging procedure benefits principally the cataloging librarians, since a catalog card for the public catalog would not have to be created for each publication the library acquired. Therefore, it saves processing time. The public is shortchanged, however, because a search for a specific document requires both the searcher's own time in the public catalog and a librarian's time in the Registration File. Whether the processing time saved outweighs the increased search time required of the user and the reference librarian should be considered by a library prior to implementing catalogs identical to those used at Makerere University College Library. Such a cost-benefit study would be of particular importance to university libraries, which often have large document collections that are used frequently.

Of course, the nonspecific "open" entries made in the public card catalog by the Makerere University College Library are in keeping with the tendency of archival classification schemes to place minimum reliance on the card catalog. With better cataloging, this classification scheme could well serve most libraries. The use of the Makerere College Library Classification's use of Library of Congress author numbers to describe the city name and document title is similar to the *Plain "J" Classification's* use of Cutter numbers to reflect department name and document title. Like the *Plain "J"* Classification, this minimal archival description of the document's bureaucratic origins allows it to escape the travails of government reorganization. The ability to use the classification notation in abbreviated form, and its applicability to documents of all types make it an attractive consideration for all libraries.

Jacquelyn Gavryck and Sara Knapp, "State Secrets Made Public," *Library Resources and Technical Services* 17 (Winter 1973): 82-92. [Documents Classification, State University of New York at Albany]

It was seen earlier in this chapter that the Rochester, New York, Public Library's documents classification made associations between government agencies and agency functions for purposes of arranging the library's publications. The classification formerly used at the State University of New York (SUNY) at Albany goes beyond that and links government agencies with subject areas. The result is a classification that cannot truly be called archival in commonly accepted terms, because it does not rely on hierarchical organization of government agencies for organization of documents. The SUNY Albany Classification is archival only in the sense that it looks to a governmental agency's area of operation in order to assign one or more subject headings which reflect the agency's function and areas) of operation.

Since documents are first grouped by geographical location before applying a subject classification, the SUNY Albany scheme is best thought of as a geographical-subject variation of the archival approach. By not using a subject area as its primary focus for document organization, it cannot be thought of as a true subject approach in the manner of schemes such as the DDC, Harvard, LC, and Glidden and Marchus.

Jacquelyn Gavryck and Sara Knapp, both librarians at SUNY Albany, have written that the scheme was developed to deal with the problem of a growing documents collection. The documents committee, which received suggestions from technical service personnel, set out to devise a scheme that would be simple, provide speedy processing, and yet not sacrifice comprehensiveness or precision. It was also important to the documents committee that the scheme have a subject approach, since it had been informally observed that users of the library, particularly undergraduate students, used a subject approach most frequently in the library.[106]

SUNY Albany's library had been assigning LC class number J85 to all United States government documents, then adding the *Superintendent of Documents Classification* number. Because of this practice, the documents committee decided to assign class number J86.2 to all state, county, and municipal documents.

It was then decided to Cutter each document twice, once for the name of the issuing state, county, or municipality, and the second time for the subject area of the document.

Cuttering documents by subject proved to be a lot of work, since the committee decided to tie the subject areas to the name of the departments and agencies from which they expected to collect documents. By contacting a number of state governments nationwide, the library acquired organizational charts of state government departments and agencies. Library of Congress Subject Headings were then assigned to agency names, based upon a guess of the probable subject area of each agency's publications.

Cutter numbers were then assigned to the subject headings. If different agencies were expected to publish documents in the same subject area, the subject headings for those agencies were assigned the same Cutter numbers. For example, the subject headings "License System" and "Liquor Laws" were both assigned the identical Cutter number of L56, since alcoholic beverage commissions and licensing departments were expected to publish documents in overlapping subject areas.

The library then created a holdings card file, which listed the assigned Cutter number and its corresponding subject heading on each card. Behind each Cuttered subject card in the holdings file were placed cards for each publication received, filed by the dual Cutter numbers. This file thus became a subject catalog, with the documents cards arranged geographically by state behind each subject heading.

The SUNY Albany library knew that the more subject headings it used in the holdings file, the more complex each search would become. Therefore, the number of subject headings assigned was limited. This decision decreased subject specificity and increased search time in cases where several subject headings had to be searched. In return, however, it provided some compensation by preserving the scheme's simplicity, and solved the problem of having many instances in which more than one subject heading Cutter number had to be assigned to agencies whose responsibilities were not limited to one subject area.

Table 29 lists some of the department names compiled by the librarians at SUNY Albany, along with the corresponding subject headings and Cutter numbers.

The subject headings SUNY Albany developed were based on activities of agencies at the state level of government. While many of them might apply to similar functions performed by agencies at the local level, a library using the classification for its local government documents collection might have to make some minor amendments to the list.

When it classified documents below the state level of government, the SUNY Albany library indicated a county publication by adding the number "2" to the Cutter number for the name of the issuing state, and indicated a municipal document by adding the number "3" to the same state Cutter number. SUNY Albany also inserted the first three letters of the city's or county's name between the state and subject Cutter numbers. Cities or counties with names such as New Orleans were abbreviated by using the first letter from the first word, and the first two letters of the second word. Table 30 illustrates two hypothetical documents as they would be classified at SUNY Albany.

Table 29.
State University of New Yorᴋ at Albany Classification—Partial Table of Department Names, Subject Headings, and Cutter Numbers

Department Names	LC Subject Headings	Subject Heading Cutter Numbers
Administration, Departments of	Administrative Agencies	A33
Aeronautics	Aeronautics	A47
Aging	Aging	A55
Air Pollution	Air-Pollution	E262
Alcoholic Beverage Control	Liquor Laws	L56
Arts	Art	A78
Banking	Banks & Banking	B35
Child Welfare & Family Services	Child Welfare	C45
Civil Defense	Civil Defense	C53
Civil Defense	See Also, Disaster Relief	E43
Commerce & Trade	Commerce	C64
Conservation & Ecology	Ecology	E26

Source: Reprinted by permission of the American Library Association from Jacquelyn Gavryck and Sara Knapp, "State Secrets Made Public: The Albany Plan" (*Library Resources & Technical Services* 17 [1] 85 and 88 [Winter 1973]).

In looking at Table 30, it has to be remembered that the first part of the call number, "J86.2," was just an arbitrary class number applied to the documents to make government documents easily recognizable. The *Plain "J"* scheme did the same thing when it used a letter J to indicate the government documents collection. Some other indicator for the documents collection could easily be used. It is also possible the SUNY Albany library might have assigned J86.2 to its government documents to eliminate any

Table 30.
State University of New York at Albany Classification—Examples of Notation

Document: Issuing Agency and Title	Notation
County of San Francisco,	J
California County Medical Center.	86.2
Statistical Survey of	C122
Medical Services Provided	SFR
to Ethnic Minorities	H83
1982	1982
City of San Francisco,	J
California.	86.2
Park Commission.	C123
Annual Park Services Report.	SRF
1982	P37
	1982

need for reclassification if it ever integrated its document collection with the main collection. The main collection, presumably, used the LC Classification.

In Table 30, the second Cutter number in the San Francisco County document, H83, represents the subject heading "Hygiene, Public." The Cutter number P37 in the San Francisco City document represents the subject heading "Parks." The notation of SUNY is a departure from other archival schemes examined, in that the issuing agency is not reflected in the notation. As mentioned before, however, the SUNY Albany scheme is not 100 percent archival.

In addition to the card provided for the holdings file, mentioned previously, the SUNY Albany Classification creates two additional catalog cards, one for agency, another for subject. One agency card is made for each agency from which documents are collected, and is filed in the main card catalog. A note on the card refers the library user to the holdings catalog in the reference department.

One catalog card is also made for each subject heading used in the documents collection. This card also refers users to the holdings catalog in the reference department. Thus, the holdings catalog is the only source which has complete information about individual documents, and is also the only complete list of all documents in the government documents collection. This situation would be inconvenient from the user's viewpoint, since it requires one look-up in the main card catalog by the users, and a second look-up by the reference librarian. The inconvenience experienced in double look-ups is a direct result of that objective of the scheme which sought speedy and simple processing. The result is a trade-off in shorter cataloging and processing time, versus longer search time. Gavryck and Knapp never stated whether the expense of such a trade-off had been estimated. The question, of course, is whether the reference librarian's time performing a search which might otherwise be made by the user is a greater or lesser expense than full cataloging and subject analysis.

In terms of rising processing costs, and the trend toward decreasing numbers of full-time staff, the difference may not be very great. Nevertheless, it is something the library's management should consider as part of the process in making such decisions. One argument for supporting the arrangement as it existed in the SUNY Albany library, is that the reference librarian, rather than the users, would have a better idea under which subject heading to look for a specific document. Knowledge of typically assigned subject headings would give the reference librarian a particular advantage in instances where a department or agency published a document outside its usual subject sphere. Knowing which of one or two subject headings were possibly assigned to a suspect document would tend to speed up search time rather than slow it down, and also increase the search-recall ratio.

Having a limited number of catalog entries also reduces the time and expense when new cross-references and main entry cards are needed because an agency changes its name, undergoes reorganization, or modifies its functions.

As the scheme was used by SUNY Albany, all publications by the same agency on the same subject have the same call numbers, and are grouped on the shelves by year of publication. In a separate collection, maintained by the reference department, potential filing and retrieval problems of duplicate call numbers could be minimized by staff awareness. In an open stack collection, retrieval might be more difficult, especially for agencies which publish considerable numbers of documents each year in the same subject areas.

Overall, this scheme is a successful blend of the subject and archival approaches to document organization, if the results are examined in light of the objectives which influenced its design. Libraries with large documents collections would probably find the SUNY Albany Classification's limited subject groupings unwieldy and its manual searches too tedious. Libraries with small collections, however, might find it a suitable solution to organizing documents at the state, interstate, commonwealth, territorial, county, and municipal government levels.

In SUNY Albany's own case, the library now fully catalogs and classifies its state and local documents according to the *Library of Congress Classification*. This was a sensible move on the part of the library because it has unified these documents with the general collection, thereby improving access and eliminating the so-called "step-child" status that government documents sometimes have. Federal government documents at SUNY

Albany are arranged according to the *Superintendent of Documents Classification*.

> Linda Siler-Regan, Charles R. McClure, and Nancy Etheredge, "Non-SuDocs Classification: A New Procedure," *Library Resources and Technical Services* 20 (Fall 1976): 361-372. [University of Texas At El Paso Classification]

The document classification scheme developed at the University of Texas at El Paso (UTEP) resulted, as have several other schemes, from an increased number of documents acquired by the university library.

In a jointly authored article, Linda Siler-Regan, then Head of the Documents, Microforms, and Map Department at UTEP, Charles McClure, formerly a History-Government librarian at UTEP, and Nancy Etheredge, formerly Head of UTEP's Documents Section, have described the development of the UTEP Classification.[107]

A number of other schemes were first examined by the library, including Swank's, Jackson's, the *Plain "J"*, and the Glidden and Marchus Classification. All were rejected as not meeting the library's objectives.

The objectives of the UTEP library were to have a documents classification that provided a unique shelf location number, with access through printed bibliographies and indexes, rather than through a subject catalog. The library intended to rely on indexes such as the *Monthly Catalog of United States Government Publications*, *Monthly Checklist of State Publications*, *United Nations Document Index*, *Public Affairs Information Service Index*, and *International Bibliography, Information, Documentation*. Additional criteria were that the scheme should be simple to apply and that a consistent method of subdivision be used under each political unit.[108]

It was decided by the Documents Committee at UTEP that mnemonics, similar to those in Jackson's Notation, should be used to indicate the level of government of each document in the collection. Table 31 lists the mnemonic codes used by the UTEP scheme.

Following the mnemonic, the UTEP scheme assigns either an acronym, a two-letter United States Postal Service abbreviation, or a generally

Table 31.
University of Texas at El Paso Classification—List of Mnemonics

I	International Documents
N	National Documents
S	State Documents
M	Municipal Documents

recognized initial abbreviation, to indicate the issuing organization, county, state, or municipality. These political unit abbreviations are separated by a hyphen from the mnemonic code. The first line of any document's notation is completed with the addition of a standard form number.

For the purposes of assigning form numbers, the committee decided to group documents into the four form subdivisions illustrated in Table 32. Serials and periodicals were given a form number because UTEP had some of its government documents filed with the periodical collection. Since it was observed that most library users looked for periodicals by title, a suggestion to Cutter government periodicals by title was approved.

Table 32.
University of Texas at El Paso Classification—Form Subdivisions

1	Serial and Periodical Publications, including reports
2	Monographs
3	Official Records
4	Reference Publications, whether published by the government organization, other governments, or commerical publishers

The standard form subdivision is always followed by a colon, to indicate a break in the classification. This feature is identical to the pattern followed in the *Plain "J"* scheme, where the document arrangement number is always followed by a colon.

The second line of the UTEP Classification's notation varies, depending upon the form of the document. Form one, Serials, Periodicals, and Reports, are always Cuttered by title. For form two, three, and four subdivsions, any official document number assigned to the publication by the issuing agency may be used. If no official document numbers are available, then form two, Monographs, are Cuttered by the name of the issuing agency and forms three and four, Official Records and Reference Publications, would be Cuttered by title.

To create a unique call number for the publication, the third line of the classification notation for all four forms of documents may use either an issue number, volume number, publication date, or accession number.

Table 33 illustrates several examples of hypothetical documents, classified by the UTEP scheme. In Table 33, the mnemonic C was used to indicate county government publications. The UTEP Classification did not assign any alphabetical letter for county publications, nor any for regional agency or foreign publications. The letters "R" and "F" could be used for the latter. This illustrates how easy it is to work modifications into classification schemes that were designed with a more limited collection in mind.

Table 33.
University of Texas at El Paso Classification—Examples of Notation

Issuing Agency and Document Title	Notation	Remarks
City of New Canaan, Connecticut. City Council. Proceedings March, 1982	M-NC 3: C83 3/1982	Cutter for Council
City of New Canaan, Connecticut. Department of Public Works. Annual Report 1982	M-NC 1: A71 1982	Cutter for Annual
City of New York. Bureau of Tourism. Fifty Places of Interest to Visit in Manhattan	M-NY 4: F466	Cutter for Fifty
Cook County, Illinois. Department of Public Health. Cook County Hospital Handbook for Nurses, Revised Ed., 1982	C-CO 2: H79 1982	Cutter for Hospital
Contra Costa County, California. Board of Supervisors. Contra Costa Monthly Journal Vol. 10, No. 2	C-CC 1: C767 10/2	Cutter for title, Contra Costa Monthly Journal

Of all archival schemes examined thus far, the UTEP Classification is akin only to the *Plain "J"* Classification, particularly the *Plain "J"* 's use of document arrangement numbers. This is because the UTEP Classification emphasizes the form of a document rather than the issuing agency's place in the governmental hierarchy. In fact, only Monographs, form subdivision two, can possibly be arranged by issuing agency—and then only if an official document number is not available. The reasons given for the emphasis on the form of the documents were ". . . to save time and money, to promote uniformity between the document collection and the library, and to allow for quicker retrieval.'' [109]

The use of form subdivisions as a principal means of organizing documents, in all likelihood, does save time and money in processing costs, when compared with schemes such as Jackson's Notation and the Dayton Classification, both of which employ a detailed enumeration of the local government's hierarchical structure. UTEP's concern with uniformity of the documents collection and the rest of the library is valid, since libraries in many instances do stress arrangement by form. Periodical and phonograph record collections are typical form arrangements.

UTEP's proposal that documents can be retrieved more quickly when arranged by form is open to question, particularly with a large documents collection. After the documents have been arranged by form, the next most common subarrangements in the UTEP scheme are official document number and title. The library user has to know either the official document number or title in order to retrieve a publication. The UTEP library would depend on indexes and bibliographies to obtain the official document number or title. While this approach might work for documents at the international, federal, and state government levels, the lack of checklists and indexes for municipal documents presents a problem at the local level. In effect, UTEP would have its users rely on *Index to Current Urban Documents*, *Public Affairs Information Service Index*, various state checklists, and newspaper references for municipal government documents. The limited coverage of those sources might be of little or no assistance in some instances. Additionally, since UTEP proposed no shelf list, there would be no record of which items were in the collection. At the time the UTEP Classification was proposed, the library appeared to have no provision for informing users of a document that was in the library's collection but was not listed in an index of some sort. It seems a fundamental error of the UTEP Classification that the library looked at retrieval only in terms of speed, without any attention to effective recall, precision, or user convenience.

There are obvious problems with this classification as applied to municipal government documents, and therefore, it cannot be recommended for use with local documents unless complemented by adequate cataloging. Even at the national government level, where indexes and catalogs of federal government documents are more numerous, UTEP still made no provision to retrieve documents acquired prior to the availability of the index in which they might be listed. There can often be a time lag of several months between the time a document is published and the time when it appears in a printed index.

The UTEP Classification has two useful advantages. The first is that it can successfully create unique document call numbers for every publication in the collection. Secondly, it is virtually 100 percent immune to governmental reorganizations or department name changes at any level of government, since government departments are hardly used in the classification process. Likewise, traces of government agencies rarely show up in the notation. Furthermore, if the classification is used in the same manner as at UTEP, that is, without use of a catalog, there also would be no need for recataloging or making new "see" references. Of course, anyone doing a retrospective search through indexes and bibliographies of government publications might face a considerable problem without reference to a record of agency name changes, particularly if no mention was made in the indexes. Unless improvements in access are made by any library considering use of the UTEP Classification, the scheme's immunity to governmental reorganization seems to be small comfort to possibly frustrated users and librarians. In fact, UTEP no longer uses the scheme. It now classes federal documents according to the *Superintendent of Documents Classification*, and state documents according to the Texas State Library's *Bordner Classification*. Local documents use an in-house scheme, based on the *Bordner*.

OTHER ARCHIVAL CLASSIFICATION SCHEMES

There are a number of additional archival classification schemes in existence, most of which are limited in focus to the arrangement of state government documents. Many of these schemes were developed to arrange the documents of a single state. The Houk scheme for Ohio documents and the Florida Atlantic University scheme for Florida state documents are two examples. The principles of organization in most of these state document schemes can be adapted or modified and applied to the archival organization of local government documents.[110] While such an adaptation may be possible for a library with a small local documents collection, libraries with large, diverse collections might find it too much of a task to broaden these sometimes narrowly focused state classifications in order to accommodate the collection at hand. In such instances, adoption of a classification such as the Makerere University College Library Classification with its ability to accommodate documents of all types would make more sense.

A SCHEME WITH COMPUTER APPLICATION

Margaret Beckman, *Automated Cataloging Systems at the University of Guelph Library*, Computerized Cataloging Systems Series (Peoria, Illinois: LARC Press, 1973).

In 1966, the government publications at the University of Guelph, in Ontario, Canada, were in a state of chaos. A sizable documents collection was scattered through several libraries, where a number of different classification schemes were in use. Not all documents were cataloged, and some were treated as periodicals. A backlog of unprocessed documents was gathering in the central processing department.

In anticipation of the construction of a new central campus library, the Chief Librarian hired Margaret Beckman to bring some order to the government documents collection by designing an automated system that would provide access to all government publications in the university's collections.[111]

By 1968 Beckman had put into operation an automated document system on the library's GEAC 800 minicomputer. The system provided quick, economical access to individual publications within the collection. Speed, economy, and the ability to handle an unlimited number of documents were three objectives at the heart of the system's development.[112]

When the University of Guelph entered into cooperative use of its computer document system with other libraries, the system took on its current acronym, CODOC, that is, Cooperative Documents.

CODOC originally was developed with the University of Guelph as the central node in a star-shaped network. As the system grew, however, concerns of member libraries to preserve individual autonomy, as well as monetary concerns of maintaining a large central union file, brought about a revision of the projected use of CODOC's union file. Instead of maintaining a uniformly cataloged union file, members decided to do their own in-house cataloging prior to placing document entries into the union file data base. A bibliographic record already entered into the union file may be used by member libraries to speed up their own in-house cataloging. While the cataloging format is standardized to a degree, CODOC's members modify the cataloging records to conform to their own in-house cataloging practices.

Today, CODOC is a consortium of eleven Ontario academic libraries. The consortium's computer union file is available for searching within Canada through CAN/OLE, the on-line search service operated by the Canada Institute for Scientific and Technical Information (CISTI), an arm of the National Research Council of Canada. Institutions located outside of Canada may obtain access to the CODOC data base through QL Systems, a Canadian bibliographic on-line search service, similar to BRS or DIALOG in the United States. Direct access by telecommunication links to the consortium's data base is possible for libraries with compatible GEAC equipment.

The fully automated CODOC system has been adopted for in-house use by other libraries in Canada outside the consortium. The only library using the full CODOC system in the United States is Stockton State College in Pomona, New Jersey. Stockton State College has entered into agreements for third-party use of its system with Rutgers University of New Brunswick, New Jersey, and Ramapo College, also in New Jersey.[113]

Margaret Beckman has emphasized that CODOC's document code is merely a shelf location device. This is an accurate description, since its shelf arrangement and classificatory structure are closely allied to the classification schemes having archival arrangements.

The CODOC system begins its arrangement and coding by assigning a two-letter alphabetical code to represent the name of the country from which a document originates. These codes are similar to the standard state abbreviations used by the United States Postal Service.

The level of government of the issuing agency within the country of origin is indicated by a single numeric character. For example, in the United States, the Arabic numeral 1 might indicate federal government documents, while 2, 3, 4, and 5 might indicate state, regional, county, and municipal documents respectively. This is a characteristic CODOC shares in common with the SUNY Albany Classification.

The number that indicates the level of government of the issuing agency is followed by another two-letter alphabetical code, which reflects the name of the state, region, county, or municipality responsible for the publication.

The issuing government department is represented, again, by a two-letter alphabetical code. Subdivisions of the government department are indicated by a two-digit number. These numbers may be assigned in sequential order and do not have to reflect any hierarchy.

The department subdivision number is followed by a hyphen and then by the last two digits of the year in which the document was published. Serials are an exception and have no publication date assigned.

The last portion of the system provides a coding option. Either a Cutter number may be used to reflect the first significant title word, or any officially assigned publication number may be employed instead. The latter option is a characteristic that has appeared in other archival schemes previously examined, such as Swank, UTEP, *Plain "J,"* and University of Makerere.

The shelf arrangement of the CODOC system organizes documents somewhat like the Makerere University College Library's documents classification. The difference is that the Makerere Classification groups documents alphabetically by city, after it has separated them by level of government, whereas CODOC groups documents alphabetically by state or province after it has separated them by level of government. With the exception of periodicals, CODOC consistently assigns the year of publication to documents as a coding facet, while the Makerere scheme opts instead for form subdivisions. Two hypothetical documents, and their corresponding CODOC document codes are illustrated in Table 34.

The CODOC document codes were structured to be easily understood and to provide a means for quick shelf location. Pearson and Hrabi have described in detail the standard coding sheets developed for CODOC document processing, a procedure that may be performed by clerical staff members. At the University of Guelph, document coding sheets are typed

Table 34.

University of Guelph, CODOC System—Examples of Document Codes

Issuing Office and Document Title	Document Code and Explanation
Dade County, Florida. Department of Streets and Highways. Personnel Office. Employee Benefits Manual, Revised edition, 1982	US3FLSH 09-82B434 The US3 is used above to indicate a document issued by a county government agency in the United States. FL is the alphabetical code for Florida, and SH is the code for Department of Streets and Highways. The Personnel Office has been assigned code 09. B434 is the Cutter number for the word Benefits in the document title.
Laredo, Texas. Tax Assessor's Office. House Lot Assessments for Laredo Estates, Tract 418 1982	US4TXTA 06-82T418 The US4 is used above to indicate a document issued by a municipal government agency in the United States. TX is the alphabetical code for Texas, and TA is the alphabetical code for the Tax Assessor's Office. 06 is a numerical code for the Tax Assessor's Office, used here because no office subunit was involved in the document's publication. T418 refers to the housing tract number.

using a special font that allows for optical character recognition by the computer's input scanning device.[114]

Even though the CODOC system is designed for computer application, its built-in flexibility allows it to be used as a manual system, supported by card files rather than an automated data base. At the University of Guelph, only two card files are maintained. One is a corporate author authority file, and the other is a series title authority file.[115] It is obvious that additional card files would have to be maintained by any library wishing to use CODOC in a manual mode. Otherwise, access to the collection would be quite limited.

The automated CODOC system produces five different and complete catalogs, arranged by corporate author, personal author, title, series, and serials listings, as well as a printed key word out-of-context (KWOC) index. In addition, the system produces a master shelf list. These catalogs were originally in the form of printouts at the University of Guelph. As paper costs escalated, however, and the size of the collection increased, the printouts were replaced with less expensive computer output microfiche (COM).[116] The University of Guelph also combined its government documents holdings with the library computer's general holdings data base, and as a result, library users may now make on-line searches for documents through the on-line inquiry catalog terminals, which provide access to the library's general collection. The general collection and CODOC data bases are actually two separate noncompatible files. The computer takes user requests and runs them through both files before producing a response.[117]

When describing the benefits of the CODOC System, the usual foci are the system's simplicity, economy, speed, unique document numbers, cost savings in allowing document processing by technicians, and its improved bibliographic control through the production of five catalogs and the KWOC title index.[118]

An additional benefit of CODOC is that its bibliographic record format, while not directly compatible with formats of other systems, can be modified so that it is compatible. This modified compatibility is true in regard to the Library of Congress's MARC record format. The ability to modify format was an important factor in the selection of the CODOC System by the library at the University of Toronto. The *Plain "J"* Classification and Rombough's *Classification Outline for Canadian Provincial Documents*, both of which were examined by the University of Toronto, were not compatible with the main data base of the library's holdings, which has used the MARC format.[119]

On the other hand, both CODOC and the Rombough Classification were rejected for use in processing government documents by the National Library of Canada (NLC). While there are similarities between CODOC and the Canadian MARC format, the latter having been adopted by the NLC, the Canadian MARC format provides for additional information about the document, such as French or English language, as well as codes for traditional subject analysis.[120]

The question of subject analysis is one of the few bones that can be picked with the CODOC System. The only subject approach to the documents is through CODOC's KWOC title index, which uses multiple key words as well as singular key words. Carolynne Presser, Assistant Librarian in the Engineering, Mathematics, and Science Library at the University of Waterloo, Ontario, believes that titles of government reports reflect recent research and current terminology and are thereby easier to retrieve by key word. William Ready and Mary Westell, both librarians at McMaster University in Hamilton, Ontario, believe that the catalogs and KWOC index produced by CODOC, along with its speed and economy in processing, outweigh ". . . the usefulness of subject analysis and full classification."[121] Both of these positions are subject to some qualification. Although it is true, as Presser pointed out, that document titles have come more and more to reflect content, particularly in the sciences, it is also true that this is not always the case. Furthermore, since terminology in the sciences and social sciences is subject to frequent change, a search in a key word index under a word in vogue in 1982 may not retrieve titles published ten years earlier, when the same topic was described by a different term. Ready and Westell may be perfectly justified in believing speed, economy, and KWOC indexing have advantages over traditional subject analysis. As far as effectiveness is concerned, however, KWIC indexes (similar to KWOC indexes) have been examined and compared to the Library of Congress Subject Headings (LCSH) by Assistant Professor Yoshiro Matsuda, of Hitotsubashi University's Documentation Centre for Japanese Economic Statistics, and by Sachiko Matsui, an assistant in the Department of Management Science at Otaru University of Commerce.

Matsuda and Matsui found that KWIC indexing generally provided more access points than LCSH. LCSH, however, provided better retrieval results when certain elements, such as dates or geographical names, were part of the search. Matsuda and Matsui also pointed out that the natural language of titles often scatters one subject described in different terms by different authors. For example, a KWIC or KWOC search for "value theory" would not retrieve a document on the same topic described in its title as "Leontief analysis." This is because, as D. J. Foskett has pointed out, KWIC and KWOC indexes have no links between related terms. Therefore, the controlled indexing vocabulary of LCSH has a retrieval advantage in situations such as the aforementioned "value theory" example, since both documents would have received the same LC subject heading.[122]

Matsuda and Matsui concluded that a "KWIC index supplemented with dates and places will be a powerful substitute for the hand-made index like LCSH." The supplementing Matsuda and Matsui mentioned is otherwise known as title enrichment among indexers and information scientists. Opportunely, title enrichment through the use of additional descriptors is a part of the CODOC System.[123] Therefore, if a library incorporates title enrichment into CODOC's KWOC index, the access it provides could be considered an adequate subject approach to any document collection.

Even with an automated approach to coding and indexing, such as CODOC, a possible stumbling block may turn out to be the inexperience on the part of the searcher. Informing the searcher to be alert to the existence of synonyms, antonyms, available thesauri, and other searching aids, is a responsiblity of the reference librarian. Bernard Fry has commented that inexperienced data base users will suffer from ". . . difficulty of direct access without aggressive and personalized reference service."[124]

OTHER ARRANGEMENTS

The seventeen classification schemes that we have examined are by no means the only methods available for organizing local government documents. Many libraries with small local document collections may find that pamphlet files are a suitable method of organization for a collection. If the collection is small, or well cataloged and indexed, there is no reason why a sequential arrangement by accession number would not serve with adequate facility.

A number of classification schemes also exist for local history materials. In some instances, a library might wish to modify or adapt its local history classification so that it can accommodate local government materials. J.P.E. Francis and Alice Alderman have described two such local history classifications, should a library prefer this approach.[125] Because the foci of these classifications are on local history, libraries should not expect to use them as they exist, without some modifications owing to regional differences in government and variations in document collection policies.

Finally, there are the so-called home-grown classification schemes which can be tailored to the particular needs of the local library more than some scheme that came into being in a remote library having different needs. Although some of the classification schemes discussed in this chapter may be in use in only a single library, libraries should be advised against developing a classification unique to their own locality and collection. It would be more advisable for librarians to work together and set standards for local government documents classification rather than have each library wander off in a different direction. Perhaps as bibliographic control of local government documents improves, standards of classification will develop as a needed by-product. This does not mean that formula arrangements will appear without any work involved. On the contrary, this area of document collection is so widespread that it will take a lot of work, particularly by public libraries and municipal archivists, to bring about acceptable standards for the organization of local government documents. There is still a long road ahead.

The reader is advised to examine the subject entry "Classification Schemes" in the Subject Index to Annotated List of Sources Consulted in the back of this book. References to other schemes not discussed here are to be found in the Annotated List of Sources Consulted.

3

Indexing of Local Government Documents

It is unfortunate, to say the least, that many of the archival classification schemes examined in the previous chapter place little or no emphasis on subject analysis of local government documents. Even CODOC, the computer-coded scheme, offers subject access only through a KWOC index. KWOC indexing falls victim to so-called "lost titles" when the title of a document is not descriptive of its contents, although the University of Guelph has maintained that the percentage of lost titles was small enough to be insignificant.[126] Those libraries that rely on KWOC or KWIC indexing may be well advised to index key words from tables of contents as well as titles, in order to take maximum advantage of the computer's manipulative abilities with these so-called free vocabularies.

As a result of poor indexing, much useful information contained in local publications remains outside the bounds of easy access. It is conceivable that reference questions sometimes go unanswered because the librarian does not know which of the publications in the local documents collection contains the answer. There are no equivalents to *American Statistical Index* and *American Statistical Abstracts* for municipal publications. D. J. Foskett has said, "Classification and indexing are two sides of the same coin."[127]

For libraries not constrained by money and the limits of LCSH, DDC, Sears, or other general subject heading lists, there are several alternate subject indexing methods, some developed especially for local government documents. Use of these headings in a separate documents catalog, whether maintained by technical services personnel, reference librarians, or documents librarians, would provide the extra access that the local documents need if they are to be used to maximum efficiency as reference tools.

Librarians who wish to improve indexing of local government publications have several subject heading lists and thesauri at their disposal. Some of these vocabularies are suitable for manual indexing methods, some for automated systems, while others are usable in either setting. For example, *Urban Affairs Subject Headings* and the revised and expanded *Contemporary Subject Headings for Urban Affairs*, developed by the publishers of *Index to Current Urban Documents*, may be used in a manual or automated indexing operation.[128]

Urban Affairs Subject Headings (UASH), was developed from several existing subject heading lists in the field of urban studies. The controlled vocabulary of UASH has been refined through use as the indexing language for *Index to Current Urban Documents*. UASH consisted of approximately two thousand terms, with scope notes and cross-references. The new edition has some 2,700 terms. Greenwood Press, the publisher of *Index to Current Urban Documents*, uses these in an automated environment. The vocabulary is equally suitable for manual card files, however.

The UASH have been published in an alphabetical list. While attempts have been made to control synonyms and to collocate related terminology in the form of subdivisions of one major term, the lack of sufficient cross-references sometimes presents a problem in determining which major terms and which related terms have been assigned to a subject. From that point of view, UASH lacks hospitality. For example, someone entering the alphabetical sequence under the terms "Dogs," "Cats," or "Pets" would find no cross-references to the officially assigned heading, "Animals, pets." In a second example, no entries or cross-references appear under the terms "Monuments," "Statues," "Civic Art," or "Art," while the term "Architecture" did not have an appropriately descriptive subdivision for civic sculpture. It was impossible to tell whether a subject heading had been assigned to this subject area without scanning the entire list. The revised and expanded *Contemporary Subject Headings for Urban Affairs* overcomes UASH deficiencies by adding more entry terms (including Sculpture) and more cross-references to related terms.

In both UASH and *Contemporary Subject headings for Urban Affairs* scope notes have been supplied parenthetically, adjacent to the appropriate terms. Form subdivisions are already supplied in many subdivisions of major terms, and it is up to the indexer to add either a geographical subdivision, a chronological subdivision, or both.

Another indexing system, Timothy C. Craven's *Nested Phrase Indexing System* (NEPHIS) is computer assisted.[129] Indexing strings, which are usually titles or title-like descriptive phrases, are created by the indexer. The indexing strings employ only four computer commands, the commands being used to manipulate the form and order of index entries. After the indexing string is written, the principle indexing task is to place caret marks around the words or terms which are to appear as index entry terms. The procedure allows indexing terms to be nested, that is, one or two terms can be used as a component part of a lengthier index phrase. Thus, an indexing string, such as "〈Budget Recommendations of 〈City Auditor〉〉" would produce two index entries on the resulting paper printout. The first entry would be under "Budget Recommendations of City Auditor," and the second would appear under "City Auditor."

The NEPHIS system is easy to learn and use. Library technician coders, after the appropriate instruction, could perform the indexing. The FORTRAN computer program for NEPHIS is cheap to run, as it requires only one input file, one output file, and 1K of core computer memory.

NEPHIS produces an index similar to a KWIC or KWOC index. Its principal advantage is that it makes it easy for the indexer to have complete control over which terms will be used as index entries, since the indexer creates the indexing strings and designates the entry terms. The computer program stop lists and other devices available in a KWIC or KWOC index do not have the ability to eliminate as many unwanted entry terms as NEPHIS does, assuming an identical amount of energy were expended on the KWIC or KWOC as on NEPHIS. In other words, access points would be reduced in number in NEPHIS, but the utility of those remaining would be greater overall, when compared with KWIC or KWOC, since the latter two are often cluttered with unwanted index entries. With NEPHIS, the indexer creates his or her own list of index terms, rather than working from a prepared list. This feature allows the authority list of approved subject headings to be as broad or as narrow as the indexer wishes. The terminology, it then follows, also can be as standard or as innovative as desired.

While NEPHIS was not specifically designed for use with government publications, it offers an automated alternative to online searching for urban information, as is available through use of the *Urban Information Thesaurus.*

The *Urban Information Thesaurus* (UIT) is an automated, post-coordinate indexing system for urban materials, including local government documents. The UIT was developed in conjunction with the establishment of the Baltimore Regional Institutional Studies Center (BRISC), an archive of governmental and private papers. With roots in the United States Department of Housing and Urban Development Library's *Urban Vocabulary* and other thesauri, the UIT provides on-line searching through a hierarchical arrangement of broad indexing terms, which have particular emphasis on planning, urban development, human services, and social history.[130] An outline of the thesaurus's hierarchy is illustrated in Table 35.

The size of the UIT vocabulary has been restricted to allow easy use by searchers and indexers who are not familiar with it. Furthermore, the UIT has allowed for integration of new subjects and terms if a library finds it necessary to amend the vocabulary. KWOC, alphabetical, and hierarchical indexes provide three entry vocabulary access pathways into the thesaurus's descriptors.

In addition to the lists of descriptors, the UIT includes two geographical

Table 35.
Urban Information Thesaurus—Outline of Hierarchy

AA0109	PHYSICAL ENVIRONMENT
AB0108	Climate
AE0105	Natural Events
AH0102	Natural Resources
AK0102	Geographic Environment
HA0108	DEVELOPMENT and INFRASTRUCTURE
HB0107	Developmental Activities
HK0101	Architecture
HM0109	Construction
HS0103	Infrastructure
HS0206	Communication and Information Systems
HT0105	Housing
HW0102	Sanitation
HX0101	Transportation
MA0102	SOCIAL ENVIRONMENT
MB0101	Cultural Activities
ME0108	Economic Activity
MK0105	Human Resources
MM0103	Population
MP0100	Information Based Processes
MS0107	Social Processes and Events
MX0105	Social Conditions
TA0100	PUBLIC AFFAIRS
TB0109	Civil Rights
TE0106	Criminal Justice
TH0103	Environmental Protection
TL0102	Health
TP0108	Manpower
TS0105	Planning
TW0104	Political and Civic Activities
TX0103	Social Welfare
WA0101	SOCIAL INSTITUTIONS
WB0100	Governmental Institutions
WE0107	Law
WE1702	Public Administration
WH0104	Executive Branch
WL0103	Judiciary
WM0102	Legislative Bodies
WS0106	Economic Institutions

Table 35 *continued*

WW0105	Management
WX0104	Business Organization
XA0108	Business Enterprises

XH0101	EDUCATION

XL0100	FAMILY

tables, one listing countries of the world and the second listing Standard Metropolitan Statistical Area names used by the United States Bureau of the Census. Also in the UIT is a list of "qualifiers," which are akin to the standard form subdivisions of other classification and indexing systems.

The UIT operates in the following manner. Each qualifier, geographical name, and thesaurus descriptor has been assigned a unique code, which may be numerical, alphabetical, or alphanumerical. As documents are received, the storage location and file numbers of the documents are tagged with as many qualifier, geographical, and descriptor codes as are thought applicable. In order to retrieve a document, a searcher uses the UIT to select the appropriate codes which best describe the type of information needed. Then, searching in a Boolean fashion, the codes which have been selected by the searcher are processed by a computer program which matches the searcher's input against coded items in the data base and makes retrievals based on correct matches. At BRISC, searching is performed using a computer processing system named ARCHON.

While UASH, *Contemporary Subject Headings for Urban Affairs*, NEPHIS, and UIT are excellent choices among the subject heading indexing vocabularies available, there are other options. Certainly *Library of Congress Subject Headings* are not to be slighted as a controlled vocabulary resource in this area. A prime consideration in using LCSH is that these are the subject headings most likely to appear on local documents which find their way into the OCLC data base, thereby making easier the potential of shared cataloging of local document bibliographic records. Of course, if LCSH are already being used by the library in question, that too, is another good reason for choosing LCSH.

Also not to be overlooked are *Urban Vocabulary*, published by the United States Department of Housing and Urban Development, *Urbandoc: A Bibliographic Information System*, prepared under the direction of Vivian S. Sessions, and thirdly, the *Draft Thesaurus in the Field of Human Settlements*, prepared by the United Nations Center for Human Settlements.[131] All three are suitable for manual or automated systems. Two advantages of using *Urban Vocabulary* are that descriptors are keyed to subject classes of the DDC and that it is revised periodically by the United States Department of Housing and Urban Development. *Urban Vocabulary* has served several times as a basis for new urban affairs thesauri, including UASH.

Urbandoc, prepared as a cooperative thesaurus project, was used as one source of reference in the compilation of UASH. It is therefore easy to think of UASH as a more refined version of *Urbandoc*. Nevertheless, *Urbandoc* is still a good, comprehensive thesaurus for indexing a basic collection of local government documents. Its three volumes present both a dictionary and key-word-in-context arrangement of descriptors.

The *Draft Thesaurus in the Field of Human Settlements* is a concise thesaurus of subject terms that could easily be applied to local government materials. Some subject areas have purposely been supplied with broad headings, although use of narrower terms by modifying the outline is possible. The major subject heading divisions are: Human Settlements Institution and Management; Settlement Planning; Housing; Building and Construction; Public Services; Transport; Community Facilities, Services; Land; Social Environment and Natural Resources; Information, Documentation; and Auxiliary Disciplines.

Another valuable indexing tool is *Urban Affairs Subject Heading Comparisons*, by Jamie R. Graham.[132] This publication is a six-column table of comparative subject headings. It was compiled as the official list of subject headings adopted by the Urban Studies Collection of the Olin Library at Washington University in St. Louis, Missouri. The table provides in alphabetical order the subject heading terms selected for use by the Olin Library, and the corresponding terms used in *Urban Vocabulary*, UASH, the Urban Affairs and Planning Thesaurus (published by the Metropolitan Council of Governments, Washington, D.C.), LCSH, and *Public Affairs Information Service* subject headings used during 1975 and 1978. In addition to providing a good basic indexing vocabulary, it could also serve as an important tool in urban planning and public administration libraries, particularly as a reference aid in preparing online data base search strategies.

If a library decided to employ in-depth subject indexing of its local document collection by means such as UASH, NEPHIS, or UIT, it might then be redundant to choose a subject shelf arrangement for its local publications. It would be more practical to complement good subject indexing with a shelf arrangement by issuing agency. A classification arrangement by agency would offer an alternate approach to finding material in the collection, as well as providing reasonably direct access to specific documents. This would facilitate access for library users who either did not need to use a subject approach, or on the other hand, wished to take advantage of the retrieval powers offered by a good classification scheme enhanced by modern indexing methods.

Notes

CHAPTER 1

1. Don Kennington, *Local Government Information in the United States of America and Canada: Report of a Study Visit in March 1979,* British Library Research and Development Report No. 5531 (London: Library Association, 1979); Kommunalt Naerdemokrati, *Redegørelese Afgivet af en Arbejdsgruppe Nedsat af Undervisningsministeriet*, 1977 (Betaenking nr. 798), cited by Ingerlise Koefoed, "The Role of the Public Library in a Grassroots Democracy: An Attempt to Provide the Public with Better Information on Local and Central Government Activities," *Scandinavian Public Library Quarterly* 10 (1977): 127; and Yuri Nakata, *Local Documents Project: Final Report to the Illinois State Library, November 15, 1976 to May 15, 1978* (Arlington, Va.: ERIC Document Reproduction Service, ED 175 394, 1978).

2. Nakata, p. 15.

3. Heywood T. Sanders, "Governmental Structure in American Cities," *Urban Data Service Report* 10 (November 1978): 2-4.

4. Lesley Grayson, "Urban Documentation: Its Nature and Purpose," *Journal of Librarianship* 7 (October 1975): 230-231.

5. Yuri Nakata, Susan J. Smith, and William B. Ernst, Jr., compilers, *Organizing a Local Government Documents Collection* (Chicago: American Library Association, 1979).

6. Ibid., p. 1.

7. Mary Kalb, "Index to Current Urban Documents," *Public Documents Highlights for Texas* 1, no. 4 (1979), cited by Michael O. Shannon, "Collection Development and Local Documents: History and Present Use in the United States," *Government Publications Review* 8A (1981): 65; and F. Brent Scollie, "Every Scrap of Paper: Access to Ontario's Municipal Records," *Canadian Library Journal* 31 (January-February 1974): 9-12.

8. Shannon, p. 69.

9. William C. Robinson, "Local Government Publications in Larger Tennessee Public and Academic Libraries," *Tennessee Librarian* 28 (Fall 1976): 122.

10. Ibid., p. 124.

11. Richard E. Moore, "Care and Retrieval of Local Documents in Public Libraries," *PNLA Quarterly* 42 (Winter 1978): 4.

12. Ibid., p. 5.

13. Shirley Hogan, "Public Libraries as Depositories of Local Government Documents," *News Notes of California Libraries* 72 (1977): 24.

14. Ibid.

15. Diane K. Harvey, "Public Access to Local Documents," *New Jersey Libraries* 11 (November 1978): 3.

16. Ibid.

17. Shannon, p. 70.

18. Terry L. Weech, unpublished paper (1982).

19. Deborah Byrne Babel, "The Effects of Type of Library on Levels of Service in Local Documents Collections" (MLS Research Paper, University of North Carolina, Chapel Hill, 1976), pp. 22-23.

20. Rebecca B. Rankin, "Bibliographical Needs in the Field of Municipal Documents," in *Public Documents*, ed. A. F. Kuhlman (Chicago: American Library Association Committee on Public Documents, 1933), p. 99.

21. Cynthia J. Durance, "Status of Cataloging Group Recommendations," *Canadian Library Journal* 37 (April 1980): 102-103.

22. Ibid.

23. Nakata, *Local Documents Project: Final Report*, p. 26.

24. Rankin, p. 100; Josephine B. Hollingsworth, "To Aid Collectors of Municipal Documents," *Special Libraries* 26 (April 1935): 87; Bernard M. Fry, *Government Publications: Their Role in the National Program for Library and Information Services* (Washington, D.C.: National Commission on Libraries and Information Science, 1978), pp. 61-62, 69-70, & 117; and Shannon, p. 63.

25. Shannon, p. 73.

26. Edith Ward, Mary Kalb, and Letitia Mutter, compilers, *Urban Affairs Subject Headings* (Westport, Conn.: Greenwood Press, 1975), p. vi.; and *Contemporary Subject Headings for Urban Affairs* (Westport, Conn.: Greenwood Press, 1983).

27. Peter Hernon, "Municipal Publications: Their Collection and Use in Reference Service," *Special Libraries* 64 (January 1973): 32.

28. Babel, p. 24.

29. Ibid., pp. 24-26.

30. Susan Folsom Berman and Karen Ann Taylor, *Municipal Publications in the Public Library: Guidelines for Collection and Organization* (Westerly, R.I.: South County Interrelated Library System, n.d.), p. 16: and T. R. Vedachalam, "Cataloging of Government Publications," *Herald of Library Science* 10 (October 1971): 357-360.

31. Bernardine E. A. Hoduski, "Critique of the Draft AACR 2nd Edition: Impact of the Rules on Documents," in *Nature and Future of the Catalog*, ed. Maurice S. Freedman and Michael S. Malinconico (Phoenix, Ariz.: Oryx Press, 1979), pp. 201-224.

32. Elaine F. Svenonius, "Directions for Research in Indexing, Classification, and Cataloging," *Library Resources and Technical Services* 25 (January 1981): 99-101.

33. Nakata, *Organizing a Local Government Documents Collection*, p. 40.

34. Ibid., pp. 40-42; and Deborah Hunt, "Publicizing the Government Documents Collection," *Unabashed Librarian*, no. 32 (1979), pp. 6-8.

35. Peter Hernon, "Academic Library Reference Service for the Publications of Municipal, State, and Federal Government: A Historical Perspective Spanning the Years up to 1962," *Government Publications Review* 5 (1978): 43-44.

36. Koefoed, pp. 129-130.

37. Robinson, p. 124.

38. Babel, pp. 20-21.

39. Nakata, *Organizing a Local Government Documents Collection,* p. 33.

40. Cheryl Winter Lewy, "Urban Documents as Reference Tools," *Illinois Libraries* 57 (April 1975): 293.

41. Benjamin Shearer, "Urban Statistical Abstract: A Guide to Local Government Documents," *RQ* 19 (Spring 1980): 236.

42. Bernard M. Fry, "Government Publications and the Library: Implications for Change," *Government Publications Review* 4 (1977): 116-117.

43. Nakata, *Local Documents Project: Final Report*, p. 15.

44. Babel, p. 32.

45. Frederic M. Miller, "The Current State of Urban Historical Documentation," *Drexel Library Quarterly* 13 (October 1977): 6.

46. Ibid., pp. 12-13.

47. Ibid., p. 10; Virginia R. Stewart and Mary Lynn Ritzenthaler, "The Constituencies of Urban Archives: Donors, Users and Institutions," *Drexel Library Quarterly* 13 (October 1977): 64-65.

48. Fry, "Government Publications and the Library," p. 114.

49. Adele M. Newburger and Paul M. Rosenberg, "Automation and Access: Finding Aids for Urban Archives," *Drexel Library Quarterly* 13 (October 1977): 49-50.

50. W. Theodore Durr and Paul M. Rosenberg, *The Urban Information Thesaurus: A Vocabulary for Social Documentation* (Westport, Conn.: Greenwood Press, 1977).

51. Newburger and Rosenberg, pp. 50-51.

52. Robinson, pp. 123-124; and Babel, p. 25.

53. Hernon, "Academic Library Reference Service," p. 46; Michael Waldo, "An Historical Look at the Debate Over How to Organize Federal Government Documents in Depository Libraries," *Government Publications Review* 4 (1977): 319-329; Mary Jane Hilburger, "The State of the Art: Bibliographic Control and Organization of Local Documents," *Illinois Libraries* 57 (April 1975): 269-271; and Yuri Nakata, *From Press to People: Collecting and Using United States Government Publications* (Chicago: American Library Association, 1979), pp. 31-36.

54. Shannon, p. 66.

CHAPTER 2

55. Robinson, p. 124; Babel, p. 25; and Nakata, *Local Documents Project: Final Report*, p. 15.

56. Melvil Dewey, *Dewey Decimal Classification and Relative Index,* Edition 19, edited under the direction of Benjamin A. Custer, 3 vols. (Albany, N.Y.: Forest Press, 1979), vol. 1: Editor's Introduction, *Introduction/Tables*, p. 1xxi.

57. Nakata, *Organizing a Local Government Documents Collection*, p. 29.

58. Gordon Stevenson, "The Historical Context: Traditional Classification Since

1950," *Drexel Library Quarterly* 10 (October 1974): 19.

59. Arnold S. Wajenberg, "MARC Coding of DDC for Subject Retrieval, *"Information Technology and Libraries* 2 (1983): 246-251.

60. Svenonius, p. 94.

61. Stevenson, p. 18.

62. James G. Williams, Martha L. Manheimer, and Jay E. Daily, eds., *Classified Library of Congress Subject Headings,* 2 vols. (New York: Marcel Dekker, Inc., 1972).

63. Svenonius, p. 95.

64. William Anderson and Sophia Hall Glidden, *A System of Classification for Political Science Collections*, Bureau for Research in Government Publication, no. 8 (Minneapolis: University of Minnesota Press, 1928).

65. Babel, p. 9.

66. Sophia H. Glidden and D. G. Marchus, *Library Classification for Public Administration Materials* (Chicago: American Library Association, 1942), pp. vii-ix.

67. Glidden and Marchus, p. 4.

68. Ibid., p. 1.

69. D. J. Haykin, review of *Library Classification for Public Administration Materials,* by Sophia H. Glidden and D. G. Marchus, *Library Journal* 67 (October 1942): 842.

70. Ralph R. Shaw, review of *Library Classification for Public Administration Materials*, by Sophia H. Glidden and D. G. Marchus, in *American Archivist* 5 (April 1942): 115.

71. Caroline Shillaber, *A Library Classification for City and Regional Planning* (Cambridge, Mass.: Harvard University Press, 1973), pp. vii-viii.

72. Ibid., p. ix.

73. Library of Congress, *Classification: Class N, Fine Arts,* 4th ed. (Washington, D.C.: Library of Congress, 1970), pp. 224-229.

74. Janet E. Armitage and Michael F. Lynch, "Articulation in the Generation of Subject Indexes by Computer," *Journal of Chemical Documentation* 7 (1967): 170-178; and Janet E. Armitage and Michael F. Lynch, "Some Structural Characteristics of Articulated Subject Indexes," *Information Storage and Retrieval* 4 (1968): 101-111.

75. Shillaber, p. 1 (opposite).

76. Vivian S. Sessions, "The City Planning and Housing Library: An Experiment in Organization of Materials," *Municipal Reference Library Notes* 37 (November 1963): 269-270.

77. Frederick N. MacMillin, *Library Classification for Special Collection on Municipal Government and Administration* (Madison, Wisc.: League of Wisconsin Municipalities, 1932).

78. National League of Cities/United States Conference of Mayors, *The NLC/USCM Library Classification System: Index for an Urban Studies Collection* (Washington, D.C.: National League of Cities/United States Conference of Mayors, 1970), p. [i].

79. Raynard Swank, *A Classification for State, County, and Municipal Documents* (Boulder: By the Author, 1941), p. 1.

80. Raynard Swank, "A Classification for State, County, and Municipal Documents," *Special Libraries* 35 (April 1944): 116.

81. Swank, *A Classification for State, County, and Municipal Documents,* p. 8.

82. Shearer, p. 236.

83. Everett J. Johnson, "Government Documents Round Table, Federal Documents Task Force Work Groups on SuDocs Classification Numbers Conference, Dallas, 1979," *Library of Congress Information Bulletin* 38 (August 1979): 362.

84. Doris Cruger Dale, "The Development of Classification Systems for Government Publications," *Library Resources and Technical Services* 13 (Fall 1969): 481.

85. Johnson, p. 362.

86. Nakata, *Local Documents Project: Final Report*, p. 15; Robinson, p. 123.

87. Linda Siler-Regan, Charles R. McClure, and Nancy Etheredge, "Non-SuDocs Classification: A New Procedure," *Library Resources and Technical Services* 20 (Fall 1976): 361-362.

88. Ellen Jackson, "A Notation for a Public Documents Classification," Library Bulletin no. 8 (Stillwater: Oklahoma Agricultural and Mechanical College, 1946), pp. 2-4.

89. Ibid., pp. 9, 14.

90. Ibid., p. 6.

91. James Rettig, "A Classification Scheme for Local Government Documents Collections," *Government Publications Review* 7A (1980): 33-34.

92. Ibid., p. 33.

93. Ibid., p. 35.

94. Thomas Heenan, "Classification of Local Publications," *Special Libraries* 65 (February 1974): 74.

95. Rettig, p. 33.

96. Heenan, p. 76.

97. Mina Pease, "The Plain 'J': A Documents Classification System," *Library Resources and Technical Services* 16 (Summer 1972): 317.

98. Library of Congress, *Classification: Class J, Political Science,* 2nd ed. (Washington, D.C.: Library of Congress, 1924; Reprinted, 1956), p. 243.

99. Pease, p. 323.

100. Library of Congress, Processing Department, *Cataloging Service Bulletin* 104 (May 1972).

101. J. Gormly Miller, "Classification of Local Municipal Documents," *Library Journal* 64 (December 1939): 938.

102. Ibid.

103. Svenonius, p. 94.

104. H. Holdsworth, "An Arrangement for Government Publications," *East African Library Association Bulletin* 1 (January 1962): 15.

105. Jacquelyn Gavryck and Sara Knapp, "State Secrets Made Public," *Library Resources and Technical Services* 17 (Winter 1973): 87.

106. Ibid., p. 83.

107. Siler-Regan, McClure, and Etheredge, pp. 361-368.

108. Ibid., p. 365.

109. Ibid., p. 370.

110. Judith Ann Houk, *Classification System for Ohio State Documents*

(Columbus: Ohio State Library, 1962); and W. L. Newsome and N. P. Sanders, "Florida Public Document Classification in the Florida Atlantic University Library," *Florida Libraries* 21 (March 1970): 27-29.

111. Ellen Pearson and Merv Hrabi, "Guelph Document System," in *Automated Cataloging Systems at the University of Guelph Library*, ed. Margaret Beckman, Computerized Cataloging Systems Series (Peoria, Ill.: LARC Press, Ltd., 1973), p. 13.

112. Virginia Gillham, "The Guelph Document System," *Government Publications Review* 7A (1980): 213.

113. Virginia Gillham, "CODOC as a Consortium Tool," *Government Publications Review* 9 (January-February 1982):48-52; William Ready and Mary Westell, "CODOC: A Canadian Cooperative Computerized Scheme for Published Government Documents," *Canadian Journal of Information Science* 3 (May 1978): 177; and Virginia Gillham, "CODOC in the 80's: Keeping Pace with Modern Technology," paper presented to the 3rd Annual Government Documents and Information Conference, Columbus, Ohio, 22-23 October 1982, pp. 10-12 & attachment.

114. Pearson and Hrabi, pp. 25-34.

115. Ibid., p. 22.

116. Gillham, "CODOC as a Consortium Tool," p. 50.

117. Gillham, "CODOC in the 80's: Keeping Pace with Modern Technology," p. 9.

118. Carolynne Presser, "CODOC: A Computer-Based Processing and Retrieval System for Government Documents," *College & Research Libraries* 39 (March 1978): 95; and Peter I. Hajnal, Valentina de Bruin, and Dale Biteen, "MARC and CODOC: A Case Study in Dual Format Use in a University Library," *Journal of Library Automation* 10 (December 1977): 361-362.

119. Gillham, "CODOC in the 80's: Keeping Pace with Modern Technology," p. 8; Hajnal, de Bruin, and Biteen, pp. 360, 362.

120. Durance, p. 103.

121. Presser, p. 97; Ready and Westell, pp. 176-177.

122. Yoshiro Matsuda and Sachiko Matsui, "Effectiveness of KWIC Index as an Information Retrieval Technique for Social Sciences," *Hitotsubashi Journal of Economics* 15 (February 1975): 24-26; and D. J. Foskett, "Problems of Indexing and Classification in the Social Sciences," *International Social Science Journal* 23 (1971) : 254.

123. Matsuda and Matsui, p. 26; Hajnal, de Bruin, and Biteen, p. 362.

124. Fry, "Government Publications and the Library: Implications for Change," p. 116.

125. Alice Alderman, *Organizing Wisconsin Public Documents: Cataloging and Classification of Documents at the State Historical Society Library* (Arlington, Va.: ERIC Document Reproduction Service, ED 176 732, 1974); and J.P.E. Francis, "Antrim's Local History Classification," *Library World* 69 (February 1968): 196-198.

CHAPTER 3

126. Joseph A. McDonald, "Guelph System," [letter in reply to R. M.

Simmons], *RQ* 12 (Summer 1973): 415.

127. Foskett, p. 253.

128. Edith Ward, Mary Kalb, and Letitia Mutter, *Urban Affairs Subject Headings* (Westport, Conn.: Greenwood Press, 1977).

129. Timothy C. Craven, "Government Publication Index Using NEPHIS [Nested Phrase Indexing System] Coding of Titles," *American Society for Information Science Journal* 28 (March 1977): 107-114.

130. Durr and Rosenberg, pp. xi-xiii.

131. United States Department of Housing and Urban Development, *Urban Vocabulary*, Revised ed. (Washington, D.C.: United States Department of Housing and Urban Development, 1975); Vivian S. Sessions, project director, *Urbandoc: A Bibliographic Information System*, 3 vols. (New York: The Graduate Division, City University of New York, 1971); and United Nations Center for Human Settlements (Habitat), *Draft Thesaurus in the Field of Human Settlements* (Nairobi: United Nations Center for Human Settlements [Habitat], 1980).

132. Jamie R. Graham, *Urban Affairs Subject Heading Comparisons* (St. Louis, Mo.: Institute for Urban and Regional Studies, Washington University, 1979).

Annotated List of Sources Consulted

*1. Alderman, Alice. *Organizing Wisconsin Public Documents: Cataloging and Classification of Documents at the State Historical Society Library.* Arlington, Virginia: ERIC Document Reproduction Service, ED 176 732, 1974.

Handbook of classification scheme used at Wisconsin State Historical Society Library. Procedures for classifying (in archival fashion) and cataloging documents of all states in the U.S., Canadian provinces, county and municipal publications of Wisconsin localities, interstate compacts, and nongovernmental publications. Adaptable for other states and cities.

*2. Anderson, William, and Glidden, Sophia Hall. *A System of Classification for Political Science Collections.* Bureau for Research in Government Publication, no. 8. Minneapolis: University of Minnesota Press, 1928.

For its time, an excellent subject classification for political science materials, including municipal government. Classes are well planned and expansive. The alphabetical index, with cross-references, is highly detailed.

*3. Armitage, Janet E., and Lynch, Michael F. "Articulation in the Generation of Subject Indexes by Computer." *Journal of Chemical Documentation* 7 (1967): 170-178.

Uses *Chemical Abstracts* entries in mock-up production of articulated subject index entries. Presents a logical model for generation of these indexes, which are based on index phrase manipulation. Discusses pros and cons.

*4. Armitage, Janet E., and Lynch, Michael F. "Some Structural Characteristics of Articulated Subject Indexes." *Information Storage and Retrieval* 4 (1968): 101-111.

Sets forth an algorithm and model for the generation of subject index entries from natural language phrases, using prepositions to organize the nouns as subject heading entries.

*5. Babel, Deborah Byrne. "The Effects of Type of Library on Levels of Service in Local Documents Collections." MLS Research paper, University of North Carolina, Chapel Hill, 1976.

National survey of local documents collections and local documents reference service in United States college and public libraries.

*An asterisk preceding an entry indicates that source was cited in the text of the book.

6. Baggett, M. "Local Documents and Public Access Workshop: A Report." *Alabama Librarian* 29 (November 1977): 8-9.

Not noteworthy reading.

*7. Beckman, Margaret. *Automated Cataloging Systems at the University of Guelph Library.* Computerized Cataloging Systems Series. Peoria, Ill.: LARC Press, 1973.

Collected articles on automated cataloging of local documents, serials, and maps, plus other automated operations at University of Guelph.

*8. Berman, Susan Folsom, and Taylor, Karen Ann. *Municipal Publications in the Public Library: Guidelines for Collection and Organization.* Westerly, R.I.: South County Interrelated Library System, Westerly Public Library, n.d.

This collecting handbook was based on guidelines developed during establishment of a collection at North Kingstown, R.I., Public Library. Of passing interest, but not as good a guide as Yuri Nakata's.

*9. Bernard, Patrick. "Government Documents Roundtable: New Developments in Documents Cataloging." *U.S. Library of Congress Information Bulletin* 39 (October 1980): 392-393.

Brief GODORT highlights in cataloging developments, such as data base usage, use of AACR2 by GPO and Library of Congress.

10. Brunner, J. Terrence. "Freedom of Information at the Local Level." *Illinois Libraries* 57 (April 1975): 271-277.

Modern information technology, Illinois law, and public access to local information are discussed.

11. Canyon, Jim. "One-Stop Information Shopping." *Nation's Cities* 10 (December 1972): 16-17.

Telephone information service at San Diego's city administration building fields questions about government on all three levels: local, state, and federal.

12. Childs, James B. "Bibliographic Control of Federal, State and Local Documents." *Library Trends* 15 (July 1966): 6-26.

Devotes three paragraphs to poor bibliographic control of municipal government documents. Mentions some checklists. Hopes for improvements.

13. Childs, James B. "Library of Congress Starts Special Municipal Collection." *Public Management* 21 (March 1939): 85-86.

Need at LC for more local documents. Calls for all municipalities to place certain records on deposit at LC.

14. Clouser, R. L., et al. "Indiana's Local Government Data Base." *State Government* 53 (Autumn 1980): 178-180.

Indiana has developed a Local Government Data Base (LGDB) to aid local government decision makers through computer analysis of data.

*15. *Contemporary Subject Headings for Urban Affairs.* Westport, Conn.: Greenwood Press, 1983.

A revised edition of UASH.

16. "Council of Ontario Universities Develops CODOC, A Computer-Based Programming and Retrieval System for the Processing and Accessing of Government Publications." *Government Publications Review* 3 (Winter 1976): 347-348.

Cites development of CODOC and lists basic features of this computer coding and cataloging system for Canadian government documents.

*17. Craven, Timothy C. "Government Publication Index Using NEPHIS Coding of Titles." *American Society for Information Science Journal* 28 (March 1977): 107-114.

Easy-to-learn and -use computer indexing system with application for government documents. Nests smaller subject headings within larger phrase subject heading entries. Needs 1K RAM to run.

18. Craven, Timothy C. "Linked Phrase Indexing." *Information Processing and Management* 14 (1978): 469-476.

Linked Phrase Indexing (LIPHIS) is similar to Nested Phrase Indexing (see entry above), but is more sophisticated.

*19. Dale, Doris Cruger. "The Development of Classification Systems for Government Publications." *Library Resources and Technical Services* 13 (Fall 1969): 471-483.

Historical development and applications of Superintendent of Documents, United Nations, Swank, Jackson, and other classification schemes at the national and international levels.

20. DeJohn, William. "Interlibrary Cooperation to Provide Access to Local Documents in Illinois: A Statewide View." *Illinois Libraries* 57 (April 1975): 286-287.

Advocacy of increased access to local documents through computer networks such as Illinois Library and Information Network (ILLINET).

*21. Dewey, Melvil. *Dewey Decimal Classification and Relative Index.* Edition 19. Edited under the direction of Benjamin A. Custer, 3 vols. Albany, N.Y.: Forest Press, 1979.

Especially see Class 352, Local Government.

22. Donahue, J. T. "Getting Local Government into the Twentieth Century Before the Twenty-First Century Arrives." *Journal of Micrographics* 11 (July 1978): 10-12.

Discusses local records management, using Cambridge, Mass., city microfilming project as an example. Implies similar techniques might be used in municipal reference libraries.

23. Duckett, R. J., ed. "YADLOGIS: A Success Story in Cooperation." *ASLIB Proceedings* 29 (April 1977): 158-167.

Cooperative selective dissemination of information service to local government officials, operated by eight libraries in Yorkshire, England. Can be used as a model for other communities.

*24. Durance, Cynthia J. "Status of Cataloging Group Recommendations." *Canadian Library Journal* 37 (April 1980): 99-107.

Recommendations involving cataloging Canadian government documents are reported, principally as they relate to inclusion in *Canadiana.*

*25. Durr, W. Theodore, and Rosenberg, Paul M. *The Urban Information Thesaurus: A Vocabulary for Social Documentation.* Westport, Conn.: Greenwood Press, 1977.

A well-formulated list of broad subject headings divided into five general hierarchical divisions. Designed for adaptability, hospitality, and computer applications in the indexing of documents from local governments and other organizations.

26. Fitter, R.S.R. "Local Government in the Libraries." *Library Association Record* 38 (September 1936): 473-474.

Common problems of local documents, i.e., lack of bibliographic control, and their value as sources of information, are topics discussed.

*27. Foskett, D. J. "Problems of Indexing and Classification in the Social Sciences." *International Social Science Journal* 23 (1971): 244-255.

Comments on KWIC, PRECIS, and principles of indexing.

*28. Francis, J.P.E. "Antrim's Local History Classification." *Library World* 69 (February 1968): 196-198.

A homemade scheme principally for local history materials. May be used as an alternative to the DDC for local documents and local history publications.

*29. Fry, Bernard M. "Government Publications and the Library: Implications for Change." *Government Publications Review* 4 (1977): 111-117.

Mainly directed to federal government documents, but examines the increasing importance of all government documents as information sources, and how libraries should handle them.

*30. Fry, Bernard M. *Government Publications: Their Role in the National Program for Library and Information Services.* Washington, D.C.: National Commission on Libraries and Information Science, 1978.

Section IV of this treatise examines responsibilities and roles of libraries and local governments in providing access to local information.

31. Gardiser, K. E. "Collecting the Elusive Local Document." *Special Libraries* 71 (April 1980): 234-236.

Means by which librarians might locate local material are discussed, along with their acquisition from local officials. Cites some bibliographic sources and checklists.

*32. Gavryck, Jacquelyn, and Knapp, Sara. "State Secrets Made Public." *Library Resources and Technical Services* 17 (Winter 1973): 82-92.

Describes the classification scheme developed for state and municipal publications at State University of New York at Albany. Scheme is based on a system of double Cuttering.

*33. Gillham, Virginia. "CODOC as a Consortium Tool." *Government Publications Review* 9 (January-February 1982): 45-53.

Describes recent developments in CODOC consortium. Gives complete bibliography of articles about CODOC.

*34. Gillham, Virginia. "CODOC in the 80's: Keeping Pace with Modern Technology." Paper presented to the 3rd Annual Government Documents and Information Conference, Columbus, Ohio, 22-23 October 1982.

After proposing better access to government publications, Gillham gives a concise overview of the CODOC system for automated processing of government documents. Mentions consortium union file, batch processing of items, and flexible format of CODOC bibliographic record.

*35. Gillham, Virginia. "The Guelph Document System." *Government Publication Review* 7A (1980): 211-216.

Gives a basic understanding of how the CODOC system for computer organization of government documents works.

*36. Glidden, Sophia Hall, and Marchus, D. G. *Library Classification for Public Administration Materials.* Chicago: American Library Association, Public Administration Service, 1942.

Classification scheme for public administration materials, using a subject approach. Designed for expansion and flexibility. Combines some aspects of DDC and LC classifications.

Haykin, D. J. "Review of *Library Classification for Public Administration Materials.*" *Library Journal* 67 (October 1942): 842.

Favorable review of Glidden and Marchus's scheme, criticizing only the logical order of some classes.

"Review of *Library Classification for Public Administration Materials*, by Sophia Hall Glidden and D. G. Marchus." *Special Libraries* 33 (April 1942): 135.

A descriptive review, without critical comment.

Sayers, W. C. Berwick. "Review of *Library Classification for Public Administration Materials*, by Sophia Hall Glidden and D. G. Marchus." *Library World* 45 (October 1942): 40-42.

Favorable words for the scheme, except to say that some classes are under-developed.

Shaw, Ralph E. "Review of *Library Classification for Public Administration Materials*, by Sophia Hall Glidden and D. G. Marchus." *American Archivist* 5 (April 1942): 114-115.

Favorable review of scheme, except to say that some areas were unevenly treated.

*37. Gormon, Michael, and Winkler, Paul W., editors, *Anglo-American Cataloging Rules*, 2nd ed. Chicago: American Library Association, 1978.

Chapter 24 explains Headings for Corporate Bodies, of particular import for local document cataloging.

*38. Graham, Jamie R. *Urban Affairs Subject Heading Comparisons.* St. Louis, Mo.: Institute for Urban and Regional Studies, Washington University, 1979.

Cross-reference index to five subject headings lists.

39. Grayson, Lesley. "British Local Government Documentation." *Government Publications Review* 3 (Fall 1976): 203-211.

Discusses the increasing awareness of local information needs. Describes problems with some standard publications, and gives suggestions for improving accessibility and bibliographic control.

*40. Grayson, Lesley. "Urban Documentation: Its Nature and Purpose." *Journal of Librarianship* 7 (October 1975): 229-251.

Excellent article on types of urban documentation, and its importance. Looks at its origin, availability, and the bibliographic control thereof. Some suggestions on how to improve document collection, i.e., identification and control, are given.

*41. Hajnal, Peter I., de Bruin, Valentina, and Biteen, Dale. "MARC and CODOC: A Case Study in Dual Format Use in a University Library." *Journal of Library Automation* 10 (December 1977): 358-373.

Experience of University of Toronto in selecting a government documents processing arrangement (CODOC) compatible with the MARC format already used by the university.

42. Harleston, Rebekah M., and Stoffle, Carla J. *Administration of Government Documents Collections.* Littleton, Colo.: Libraries Unlimited, Inc., 1974.

Chapter 9 discusses the Library of Congress, Dewey Decimal, Swank, Jackson, and Plain "J" classifications in the context of federal government documents, the latter being the focus of the book.

*43. Harvey, Diane K. "Public Access to Local Documents." *New Jersey*

Libraries 11 (November 1978): 3-5.

News notes of work by Government Documents Association of New Jersey in improving access to local documents, and position paper which calls for a uniform system of depositories for local government documents.

44. Hatcher, Ruth C., "The Municipal Documents Collection at the Queens Borough Central Library: A Description." MA Report, Long Island University, Greenvale, N.Y., 1969.

Summary of the New York City Municipal Reference Library document situation. Describes the series of documents maintained by the Queens Borough branch of the New York Municipal Reference Library.

*45. Haykin, D. J. See citation at entry 36, Glidden, Sophia Hall.

*46. Heenan, Thomas. "Classification of Local Publications." *Special Libraries* 65 (February 1974): 73-76.

Describes a classification for local government publications arranged hierarchically by agency, and based on a key city principle.

*47. Hernon, Peter. "Academic Library Reference Service for the Publications of Municipal, State, and Federal Government: A Historical Perspective Spanning the Years up to 1962." *Government Publications Review* 5 (1978): 31-50.

Gives little attention to municipal documents. Examines reasons behind irregular reference service, and proposes further avenues of study on the question.

*48. Hernon, Peter. "Municipal Publications: A Bibliographic Guide to Library Literature." *Government Publications Review* 5 (1978): 445-453.

Annotated list of ninety-nine articles, books, and other publications related to municipal documents, listed in *Library Literature* through 1977. Classified subject arrangement.

*49. Hernon, Peter. "Municipal Publications: Their Collection and Use in Reference Service." *Special Libraries* 64 (January 1973): 29-33.

Deals less with reference service than with acquisition problems and lack of bibliographic control.

50. Hernon, Peter, and Aluri, R. "Municipal Publications: A Selective Bibliographic Guide to 153 Cities." *Government Publications Review* 2 (Spring 1975): 127-165.

Many of the 153 libraries that responded to this questionnaire survey also list their documents in *Index to Current Urban Documents.* Alphabetical arrangement by state and city.

51. Hernon, Peter, et al., eds. *Municipal Government Reference Sources: Publications and Collections.* New York: Bowker, 1978.

Selected guide to local documents collections in the United States.

52. Hilburger, Mary Jane. "Selected Bibliography on Local Documents." *Illinois Libraries* 57 (April 1975): 291-292.

Annotated list of fourteen selected journal articles, published between 1959 and 1974. All but three overlap with Hernon's bibliography in entry 48 of this list of sources.

*53. Hilburger, Mary Jane. "The State of the Art: Bibliographic Control and Organization of Local Documents." *Illinois Libraries* 57 (April 1975): 269-271.

Author, reference librarian at Chicago Municipal Reference Library, describes local documents in Chicago.

*54. Hoduski, Bernardine E. A. "Critique of the Draft AACR, 2nd Edition: Impact of the Rules on Documents Cataloging." In *Nature and Future of the*

Catalog, edited by Maurice J. Freedman and Michael S. Malinconico. Phoenix, Arizona: Oryx Press, 1979. Pp. 201-224.

Discusses AACR2's increased use of personal author (vs. corporate body) as a main entry.

55. Hoffman, Helen. "The Cataloging of Microform." *Australian Special Libraries News* 11 (March 1978): 17-19.

Access to microforms through card catalogs and bibliographies, and some options for cataloging and classification are discussed.

*56. Hogan, Shirley. "Public Libraries as Depositories of Local Government Documents." *News Notes of California Libraries* 72 (1977): 23-24.

Local document organization, arrangement, classification, indexing, and depository status at Sacramento City-County Library.

*57. Holdsworth, H. "An Arrangement for Government Publications." *East African Library Association Bulletin* 1 (January 1962): 15-25.

Scheme described for classification of documents at all levels of government, used at Makerere University College Library. Incorporates elements of United Nations and Library of Congress classifications.

58. Hollingsworth, Josephine B. "Responsibility of the Library for Conservation of Local Documents." *Special Libraries* 24 (August 1977): 146-148.

Notes union lists of local documents being prepared in Los Angeles and San Francisco. Suggests a regional system of libraries to collect local documents on a nationwide basis.

*59. Hollingsworth, Josephine B. "To Aid Collectors of Municipal Documents." *Special Libraries* 26 (April 1935): 86-87.

Effort to initiate exchanges of local documents between cities. Notes increase in documents during the Depression, and several union lists and checklists that have been completed.

*60. Houk, Judith Ann. *Classification System for Ohio State Documents.* Columbus: Ohio State Library, 1962.

An archival classification scheme for Ohio state documents.

*61. Hunt, Deborah. "Publicizing the Government Documents Collection." *Unabashed Librarian* no. 32 (1979): 6-8.

Presents several techniques to bring public attention to the local documents collection, such as exhibits, television and radio announcements, and freebie tables.

62. Hyman, Richard J. "Shelf Classification Research: Past, Present, Future?" Graduate School of Library Science Occasional Paper 146, University of Illinois at Champaign-Urbana, 1980.

Examines research in shelf arrangement of books. Notes trends, such as title and numerical shelving practices, in the 1970s in United States and abroad. Also available from ERIC, ED 197 741.

63. Irvine, Elizabeth. "Information Services for the Local Authority: The Public Librarian's Response." *An Leabharlann* 8 (Winter 1979): 23, 25-27, 29-31.

Use of selective dissemination of information to local government (British and Irish) officers and counselors to help define public library's information role in the community.

64. Irving, Ann. "Libraries' Central Role in Informing the Community." *Library Association Record* 80 (January 1978): 11.

Local librarians have joined with local radio broadcasters to gather local information in all forms, and provide access thereto.

65. Jackson, Ellen Pauline. "Cataloging, Classification and Storage in a Separate Documents Collection." *Library Trends* 15 (July 1966): 50-57, 58-71.

Focuses principally on the problem of cataloging publications of government agencies which are the subjects of reorganization or name change. Federal documents only.

*66. Jackson, Ellen Pauline. "A Notation for a Public Documents Classification." Library Bulletin no. 8. Stillwater: Oklahoma Agricultural and Mechanical College, 1946.

A notation, not a classification scheme, says Jackson, which allows for agency-alphabetical arrangement of federal, state, county, local, international, and foreign documents. Incorporates some features of Superintendent of Documents and Swank classifications.

67. Jackson, Isabel H. "Advantages and Disadvantages of a Subject System of Classification as Key to a Depository Collection." *College & Research Libraries* 12 (January 1951): 42-45.

Results of three surveys asking how libraries organized and classed their government publications, and whether they were satisfied with the particular method used. Mostly federal documents.

*68. Johnson, Everett J. "Government Documents Round Table, Federal Documents Task Force Work Group on Superintendent of Documents Classification Numbers Conference, Dallas, 1979." *Library of Congress Information Bulletin* 38 (August 1979): 361-363.

Report of papers presented at GODORT's midwinter meeting, examining problems of Superintendent of Documents Classification.

69. Jones, Houston G. *Local Government Records: An Introduction to Their Management, Preservation, and Use.* Nashville, Tenn.: American Association for State and Local History, 1980.

Addresses official records more than it does local documents. Perspective is that of the archivist and relationship to a records management program.

*70. Kennington, Don. "Local Government Information in the United States of America and Canada: Report of a Study Visit in March 1979." British Library Research and Development Report 5531, Library Association, 1979.

Tour of libraries, publishers, and other organizations in the local documents sphere, as reported by visiting British librarians. Stops in Washington, D.C., Chicago, Toronto, Boston, and New York City.

71. Kerschner, Joan. "State and Local Documents Microfilming Programs." *Microform Review* 7 (September-October 1978): 268-270.

Describes the *Index to Current Urban Documents* Microfiche Program, and State of Nevada's low-cost method of microfilming local documents. Mentions other state programs.

72. Kerschner, Joan G. "State and Local Publications in Microform." *Microform Review* 8 (Fall 1979): 272-274.

Lists publishers of state and local documents in microformat.

*73. Koefoed, Ingerlise. "The Role of the Public Library in a Grassroots Democracy: An Attempt to Provide the Public with Better Information on Local and Central Government Activities." *Scandinavian Public Library Quarterly* 10 (1977): 125-130.

Describes Danish Information Ministry's report that public libraries should serve as community information centers. Describes local information experiment at Lyngby Public Library.

74. Kraemer, Kenneth L., and King, John Leslie. "Development of Urban Information Systems: Status and International Relevance of United States Experience." *International Review of Administrative Sciences* (Brussels) 44 (1978): 221-232.

Growing use of computer information systems in urban areas throughout the nation. Reports data gathered by Urban and Regional Information Systems Association (URISA), and describes URBIS project.

*75. Lewy, Cheryl Winter. "Urban Documents as Reference Tools." *Illinois Libraries* 57 (April 1975): 292-298.

Stresses the most common types of municipal documents and their contents.

*76. Library of Congress. *Classification: Class J, Political Science,* 2nd ed. Washington, D.C.: Library of Congress, 1924; Reprinted 1956.

Class JS13, and following, include mayor's and departments' reports, council proceedings, and ordinances. It also provides the foundation for the Plain "J" Classification (see Pease, Mina, in this list of sources consulted).

*77. Library of Congress. *Classification: Class N, Fine Arts.* 4th ed. Washington, D.C.: Library of Congress, 1970.

Geographical Table II from this edition was used in Caroline Shillaber's revision of the Harvard Graduate School of Design Classification.

*78. Library of Congress. Processing Department. *Cataloging Service Bulletin* 104 (May 1972).

Revised Library of Congress author numbers.

79. Library of Congress. Processing Department. "Statement on Access Points for Microforms." *Microform Review* 7 (March 1978): 73-74.

Differences in cataloging of microforms, AACR1 versus AACR2. Soliciting of opinions from libraries. Lists elements to be considered in text of catalog card description and MARC format.

80. "Local Government Document Access." *Library Association Record* 82 (July 1980): 303.

News item of a two-day seminar directed by Don Kennington. Discussions included improving information transfer and local government documentation management. Article does not summarize those discussions, just reports them.

81. Lovgren, Amy. "Major Monographic Literature for Government Documents Librarians: A Selected Classified Bibliography 1900-Mid 1978." *Government Publications Review* 6 (1979): 37-46.

Includes a table indicating whether each article cited discusses federal, state, or local documents. Includes 106 unannotated entries in six subject areas. Of thirteen entries concerning local documents, only one entry overlaps with Hernon's bibliography of local materials, entry 48 in this list.

82. Marshall, S. H. "A Modern Records Management Program." *Municipal Finance* 42 (November 1969): 85-90.

Review of Fort Lauderdale, Florida's, records management program, and related state law.

*83. Matsuda, Yoshiro, and Matsui, Sachiko. "Effectiveness of KWIC Index as an Information Retrieval Technique for Social Sciences." *Hitotsubashi Journal of Economics* 15 (February 1975): 15-40.

KWIC indexing offers more access points, but effectiveness depends on keyword context dependency and user's insight, this study reports.

*84. MacMillin, Frederick N. *Library Classification for Special Collection on Municipal Government and Administration.* Madison, Wisc.: League of Wisconsin Municipalities, 1932.

A usable, expandable decimal classification scheme that needs modification, updating, and an alphabetical index.

*85. McDonald, Joseph A. "Guelph System." *RQ* 12 (Summer 1973): 415-416.

Letter to the editor in reply to R. M. Simmons. Describes early history of University of Guelph document system.

86. Milick, Patricia S. "The Answer Van in Rural New Jersey." *Library Journal* 103 (May 1978): 1030-1031.

Van is used to publicize municipal ordinances and provide I&R services.

*87. Miller, Frederic M. "The Current State of Urban Historical Documentation." *Drexel Library Quarterly* 13 (October 1977): 1-15.

Close look at urban archives in Houston and Philadelphia.

88. Miller, Frederic M., ed. "Documenting Urban Society." *Drexel Library Quarterly* 13 (October 1977): 1-123.

Entire issue of nine articles devoted to urban documentation.

*89. Miller, J. Gormly. "Classification of Local Municipal Documents." *Library Journal* 64 (December 1939): 938-941.

Describes classification for local documents used by Rochester, New York, Public Library, a system based on organization by governmental function.

*90. Moore, Richard E. "Care and Retrieval of Local Documents in Public Libraries." *PNLA Quarterly* 42 (Winter 1978): 4-6.

Discusses effect of P.L. 93-502 in terms of increased interest in local government information. Brief descriptions of acquisition, cataloging, classifying, circulating, and archival storage.

91. Morgan, Candace, ed. "Local Documents." *Illinois Libraries* 57 (April 1975): 247-304.

Entire issue is a compilation of papers presented at a local documents workshop in Chicago.

92. Mueller, Beth. "Interlibrary Cooperation to Provide Access to Local Documents in Illinois: A System View." *Illinois Libraries* 57 (April 1975): 288.

Advocates union lists and cooperative interlibrary loan of local documents.

93. Myers, Judy E., and Britton, Helen H. "Government Documents in the Public Card Catalog: The Iceberg Surfaces." *Government Publications Review* 5 (1978): 311-314.

Lists advantages and disadvantages of main card catalog entries for government documents.

*94. Nakata, Yuri. *From Press to People: Collecting and Using United States Government Publications.* Chicago: American Library Association, 1979.

Overview of federal government documents collections, from printing through acquisition, organization, classification, and reference service.

*95. Nakata, Yuri. *Local Documents Project: Final Report to the Illinois State Library, November 15, 1976 to May 15, 1978.* Arlington, Va.: ERIC Document Reproduction Service, ED 175 394, 1980.

Report on methodology and results of Illinois State Library Local Documents

Project, which was designed to create an awareness of local documents among librarians, and gather information about collections in Chicago metropolitan area.

*96. Nakata, Yuri; Smith, Susan J.; and Ernst, William B., Jr. *Organizing a Local Government Documents Collection.* Chicago: American Library Association, 1979.

This manual was a product of the Illinois State Library Local Documents Project, a federally funded study directed by Yuri Nakata. Very good basic, detailed introduction to collecting and housing a local documents collection.

*97. Nakata, Yuri, and Strange, Michele. *Classification Scheme for Illinois State Publications: As Applied to the Documents Collection at the Library, University of Chicago at Chicago Circle.* Champaign: University of Illinois, 1974.

Archival arrangement for Illinois state documents. Has alphabetical index.

*98. National League of Cities/United States Conference of Mayors. *The NLC/USCM Library Classification System: Index for an Urban Studies Collection.* Washington, D.C.: National League of Cities/United States Conference of Mayors, 1970.

Provides a Dewey-like subject arrangement for urban documentation. Somewhat wanting in index cross-references and systematic arrangement.

*99. Newburger, Adele M., and Rosenberg, Paul M. "Automation and Access: Finding Aids for Urban Archives." *Drexel Library Quarterly* 13 (October 1977): 45-59.

Explores use of computer in providing access to local documents, with particular reference to the ARCHON on-line search system at the Baltimore Region Institutional Studies Center.

*100. Newsome, Walter L., and Sanders, Nancy P. "Florida Public Document Classification in the Florida Atlantic University Library." *Florida Libraries* 21 (March 1970): 27-29.

Archival scheme for Florida state documents.

101. Norris, D. M. "Local Collections: Some Problems of Classification and Cataloguing." *Library World* 69 (February 1968): 193-196.

Generally discusses classification problems and then looks at specific difficult materials, such as maps.

102. Palmer, Forrest C. "Simmons vs. Schwarzkopf: The Great Classification Debate," *Southeastern Librarian* 27 (Fall 1977): 163-166.

Continuing discussion about how to handle documents emanating from a reorganized government bureau.

*103. Pearson, Ellen, and Hrabi, Merv. "Guelph Document System." In *Automated Cataloging Systems at the University of Guelph Library,* ed. Margaret Beckman. Computerized Cataloging Systems Series. Peoria, Illinois: LARC Press, Ltd., 1974.

With facsimile examples, describes the minute coding details of document processing with the CODOC system.

*104. Pease, Mina. "Plain 'J': A Documents Classification System." *Library Resources and Technical Services* 16 (Summer 1972): 315-325.

A classification scheme for international, federal, state, regional, local and nongovernmental documents, based on Library of Congress Classification's Class J.

105. Pinkney, Gertrude. "DPL and MRL: The Ties That Bind." *Government Publications Review* 2 (1975): 359-361.

Origin and operations of the Municipal Reference Library, part of the Detroit Public Library.

106. Presser, Carolynne. "Canadian Provincial and Municipal Documents: The Mystery Explained." *Government Publications Review* 2 (Winter 1975): 17-25.

Current status of bibliographic control, or lack of it, for Canadian local documents. Explains modified Guelph (CODOC) classification system used at University of Waterloo.

*107. Presser, Carolynne. "CODOC: A Computer-Based Processing and Retrieval System for Government Documents." *College & Research Libraries* 39 (March 1978): 94-98.

Describes cooperative computer cataloging of government documents by Ontario library network.

108. Preston, Tony, " 'GREMLIN' . . . A Comparative Local Government Information Service." *ASLIB Proceedings* 31 (May 1979): 258-260.

Ten greater Manchester, England, libraries have pooled resources to develop a monthly current awareness service for local government officials.

*109. Rankin, Rebecca B. "Bibliographic Needs in the Field of Municipal Documents." In *Public Documents,* ed. A. F. Kuhlman. Chicago: American Library Association Committee on Public Documents, 1933. Pp. 95-100.

Recants number of titles published and cites lack of bibliographic control. Suggests regional checklists and local depository status to achieve bibliographic control.

*110. Ready, William, and Westell, Mary. "CODOC: A Canadian Cooperative Computerized Scheme for Published Government Documents." *Canadian Journal of Information Science* 3 (May 1978): 176-180.

Provides an overview of the Canadian Cooperative computerized scheme for published government documents (CODOC), as it existed in early 1978.

111. Reining, Henry, Jr. "More Libraries for City Halls." *National Municipal Review* 24 (August 1935): 448-454.

Brief history of municipal reference libraries and their services. Thinks potential of the municipal reference library is to be an intelligence unit for the city, citizens, and citizens' groups.

*112. Rettig, James. "A Classification Scheme for Local Government Documents Collections." *Government Publications Review* 7A (1980): 33-39.

Archival scheme developed for local documents at University of Dayton.

113. "Review of *Library Classification for Public Administration Materials.*" See citation at entry 35, Glidden, Sophia Hall.

*114. Robinson, William C. "Local Government Publications in Larger Tennessee Public and Academic Libraries." *Tennessee Librarian* 28 (Fall 1976): 121-128.

Overview of documents collection problems. Reports results of questionnaire survey of Tennessee public and university library local document collections; compares findings to Nakata's Chicago-area survey.

*115. Rombough, Beatrice C., compiler. *Classification Outline for Canadian Provincial Documents.* Kingston, Ontario: Queen's University, Douglas Library, n.d.

Classification scheme for Canadian government documents.

*116. Sanders, Heywood T. "Governmental Structure in American Cities."

Urban Data Service Report 10 (November 1978): 1-14.

Details the most common types of city governments, and the shift toward council-manager form.

*117. Sayers, W. C. Berwick. See citation at entry 35, Glidden, Sophia Hall.

118. Schneider, Kathy. "Who's Responsible Here? Local Government Documents." *Wisconsin Library Bulletin* 73 (November 1977): 291.

Concise article describing importance of acquiring local documents by public libraries, and how to go about collecting them.

*119. Scollie, F. Brent. "Every Scrap of Paper: Access to Ontario's Municipal Records." *Canadian Library Journal* 31 (January-February 1974): 8-16.

Explains types of documents produced by local Canadian municipalities. Cites lack of municipal records management programs, poor bibliographic control. Makes recommendations for improving both bibliographic control and records management.

*120. Sessions, Vivian S. "City Planning and Housing Library: An Experiment in Organization of Materials." [Municipal Reference Library] *Notes* 37 (November 1963): 269-283.

A limited classification scheme that arranges materials first geographically, then by subject and form.

*121. Sessions, Vivian S., proj. director. *Urbandoc: A Bibliographic Information System.* 3 vols. New York: the Graduate Division, City University of New York, 1971.

Thesaurus of descriptors for urban information.

*122. Shannon, Michael O. "Collection Development and Local Documents: History and Present Use in the United States." *Government Publications Review* 8A (1981): 59-87.

A wide-ranging and informative article on the current status of municipal document publication, bibliographic control, and collection in the United States.

123. Shannon, Michael O. "For the Control of Municipal Documents." *Special Libraries* 61 (March 1970): 127-130.

Discusses overdue need for bibliographic control. Lists some state document checklists, and explains bibliographies of municipal documents prepared by New York Pubic Library's Economic Division.

*124. Shaw, Ralph R. See citation at entry 35, Glidden, Sophia Hall.

*125. Shearer, Benjamin F. "*Urban Statistical Abstract*: A Guide to Local Government Documents." *RQ* 19 (Spring 1980): 231-236; Discussion. *RQ* 20 (Fall 1980): 108-109.

Story of St. Louis University Library's effort in using federal, state, and local government publications to compile a St. Louis area statistical index similar to *American Statistics Index.* Reply by Mary Kalb, *Index to Current Urban Documents,* editor.

*126. Shillaber, Caroline. *A Library Classification for City and Regional Planning.* Cambridge, Mass.: Harvard University Press, 1973.

Classification scheme, plus index, developed at Harvard for local planning publications and other urban studies documents.

*127. Siler-Regan, Linda; McClure, Charles R.; and Etheredge, Nancy. "Non-SuDocs Classification: A New Procedure." *Library Resources and Technical Services* 20 (Fall 1976): 361-372.

Looks at principles of several document classification schemes, then describes a scheme devised for the University of Texas at El Paso Library, which classes documents at all levels of government.

128. Stallings, C. Wayne. "Local Information Policy: Confidentiality and Public Access." *Public Administration Review* 34 (May-June 1974): 197-204.

Discusses continuing conflict between public access and confidentiality of information in local records, with particular emphasis on electronically stored data.

129. "State and Local Documents in a University Library: A Symposium." *Library Journal* 61 (June 1936): 445-447, 478-480.

Recants position that bibliographic control is poor at local level. Lists four means of acquisition: begging, buying, exchanging, and gifts.

130. State University of New York, Albany. School of Library Science. *Schenectady County: A Guide to the Municipal Records.* Arlington, Va.: ERIC Document Reproduction Service, ED 142 171, 1977.

Compilation of municipal government documents bibliography by students in a seminar given by Joe Morehead. Basically an inventory of holdings in all city and county agencies. Pages ii-iv list organizations and agencies to include when inventorying.

*131. Stevenson, Gordon. "The Historical Context: Traditional Classification Since 1950." *Drexel Library Quarterly* 10 (October 1974): 11-20.

Impact of automation on traditional classification schemes, such as Dewey Decimal and Library of Congress, is discussed.

*132. Stewart, Virginia R., and Ritzenthaler, Mary Lynn. "The Constituencies of Urban Archives: Donors, Users and Institutions." *Drexel Library Quarterly* 13 (October 1977): 60-75.

Overview of urban archives.

133. Streatfield, David. "Information in Social Services Departments." *Social Service Quarterly* 51 (July-September 1977): 5-9.

Acquisition and transmission of information by employees in twenty-one British social services departments. Also describes a selective dissemination of information service for social workers. Informative.

*134. Svenonius, Elaine F. "Directions for Research in Indexing, Classification, and Cataloging." *Library Resources and Technical Services* 25 (January 1981): 88-103.

Discusses theory of "aboutness." Expresses opinion on need for more theoretical research, rather than evaluative or practical.

*135. Swank, Raynard. "A Classification for State, County, and Municipal Documents." *Special Libraries* 35 (April 1944): 116-120.

Method of classifying government documents according to provenance, with little reliance on cataloging.

*136. Swank, Raynard. *A Classification for State, County, and Municipal Documents.* Boulder, Colo., 1941.

Arranges documents by provenance and type of publication. Developed while Swank was librarian at University of Colorado, Boulder.

137. Thompson, Enid T. *Local History Collections: A Manual for Librarians.* Nashville, Tenn.: American Association for State and Local History, 1978.

Although directed toward local history materials, contains some valuable information, particularly about document conservation.

138. Tripp, Pat. "Audiocassettes for Local Government Information." *Assistant Librarian* 70 (January 1977): 6-7.

Librarians provide cassettes to local government officers and counselors. Cassettes contain general survey or analysis of unfamiliar topic or piece of legislation.

139. Tripp, Pat. "On the Tracks of Municipal Government Publications in Canada." *Canadian Library Journal* 28 (November-December 1971): 464-467.

Somewhat dated discussion of growth of interest in Canadian municipal information, lack of bibliographic control. Notes some sources and projects which are attempting control.

*140. United Nations Center for Human Settlements (Habitat). *Draft Thesaurus in the Field of Human Settlements.* Nairobi: United Nations Center for Human Settlements (Habitat), 1980.

Thesaurus of descriptors for urban information.

141. United States Civil Service Commission. *Library Arrangement of Public Administration Materials.* Washington, D.C.: United States Civil Service Commission Library, 1945.

Elementary subject headings for public administration materials. Narrow in scope, and not as useful as Glidden and Marchus scheme and index.

*142. United States Department of Housing and Urban Development. *Urban Vocabulary.* Rev. ed. Washington, D.C.: United States Department of Housing and Urban Development, 1975.

*143. Vedachalam, T. R. "Cataloguing of Government Publications." *Herald of Library Science* 10 (October 1971): 356-368.

Supports main entry under name of corporate body, with a nominal entry under subject.

144. Waidelich, Ann. "Information/Reference Service from Local Documents: A Case Study." *Illinois Libraries* 57 (April 1975): 280-285.

Madison, Wisconsin, Municipal Reference Librarian explains bibliographic control, accessibility, and information service for local government information in Madison and Dane counties.

*145. Wajenberg, Arnold S. "MARC Coding of DDC for Subject Retrieval." *Information Technology and Libraries* 2 (September 1983): 246-251.

Numerical coding of MARC tapes with elements of DDC classification numbers would allow potential Boolean searching on DDC's facets.

*146. Waldo, Michael. "An Historical Look at the Debate Over How to Organize Federal Government Documents in Depository Libraries." *Government Publications Review* 4 (1977): 319-329.

Separate versus integrated collections. Discussion limited to federal government documents, but has parallels with local documents.

*147. Ward, Edith; Kalb, Mary; and Mutter, Letitia, compilers. *Urban Affairs Subject Headings.* Westport, Conn.: Greenwood Press, 1975.

Alphabetical list (index) of subject headings used in *Index to Current Urban Documents.*

148. Weinberg, Allen. "Municipal Archives and the Philadelphia Paradigm." *Drexel Library Quarterly* 13 (October 1977): 34-44.

Explains Baltimore Region Institutional Studies Center, a regional urban archive.

*149. William, James G.; Manheimer, Martha L.; and Daily, Jay E., eds. *Classified Library of Congress Subject Headings.* 2 vols. New York: Marcel Dekker. Inc., 1972.

A good attempt at organizing Library of Congress Subject Headings for computer subject searches.

150. Zabrosky, Frank A. "The Records of Urban Society." *Drexel Library Quarterly* 13 (October 1977): 16-33.

Describes efforts to collect urban documents at Hillman Library, University of Pittsburgh.

Subject Index to Annotated List of Sources Consulted

AACR2, 37 (Gorman), 54 (Hoduski)

Access to information, public, 10 (Brunner), 20 (DeJohn), 30 (Fry), 43 (Harvey), 64 (Irving), 73 (Koefoed), 80 (n.a.), 92 (Mueller)
  automated, 99 (Newburger and Rosenberg), 128 (Stallings)
  maintaining confidentiality, 128 (Stallings)

Acquisition, 5 (Babel), 6 (Baggett), 31 (Gardiser), 40 (Grayson), 49 (Hernon), 64 (Irving), 90 (Moore), 96 (Nakata), 114 (Robinson), 118 (Schneider), 122 (Shannon), 128 (Stallings), 150 (Zabrosky)

Archives, urban, 22 (Donahue), 29 (Fry), 69 (Jones), 87 (Miller), 88 (Miller), 90 (Moore), 99 (Newburger and Rosenberg), 132 (Stewart), 148 (Weinberg), 150 (Zabrosky)

Arrangement of documents, 56 (Hogan), 62 (Hyman)
  separated versus integrated, 47 (Hernon), 65 (Jackson), 146 (Waldo)

Automated cataloging and classification, 7 (Beckman), 16 (n.a.)

Automated indexing, 17 (Craven), 18 (Craven)

Availability, of local government information, 40 (Grayson)

Bibliographic control, 5 (Babel), 30 (Fry), 40 (Grayson), 122 (Shannon), 123 (Shannon), 129 (n.a.)
  bibliography of, 48 (Hernon)
  Canada, 24 (Durance), 106 (Presser), 119 (Scollie), 139 (Tripp)
  centralized versus decentralized, 5 (Babel), 58 (Hollingsworth)
  checklists, 8 (Berman), 12 (Childs), 31 (Gardiser), 44 (Hatcher), 59 (Hollingsworth), 109 (Rankin)
  Chicago Municipal Reference Library, 53 (Hilburger)
  computer networks, 5 (Babel), 92 (Mueller), 139 (Tripp)
  England, 39 (Grayson)
  lack of, 12 (Childs), 13 (Childs), 26 (Fitter), 109 (Rankin)
  Madison, Wisconsin, 144 (Waidelich)
  problems, 5 (Babel), 39 (Grayson), 47 (Hernon), 123 (Shannon)
  union lists, 58 (Hollingsworth)

This index cites item number, not page number; n.a. = no author

Index